RAILWAYS
Then and Now

The Changing Railway Scene in Britain

To my father, Captain Alfred George Course,
Master Mariner and Author, 1895–1976

RAILWAYS
Then and Now

Edwin Course

Book Club Associates

London

By the same author:
London Railways (*Batsford, 1962*)
The Railways of Southern England: The Main Lines (*Batsford, 1973*)
The Railways of Southern England: Secondary and Branch Lines (*Batsford, 1974*)
The Railways of Southern England: Independent and Light Railways (*Batsford, 1976*)

Printed in Great Britain

First published 1979
© Edwin Course 1979

This edition published 1979
by Book Club Associates.
By arrangement with B.T. Batsford Ltd.

Contents

Sources & Acknowledgments

Acknowledgments for photographs

The author and publishers would like to thank the following for the photographs, with apologies for anybody we have been unable to trace: A.W. Burges 77, 160. H.C. Casserley 1, 17, 70, 85, 96, 123, 127, 131, 173, 175, 179, 215, 230, 238, 249. R.M. Casserley 27. F. Church 99, 103, 107, 110, 116, 118, 120, 121, 125, 136, 137, 158, 183, 222, 261. J.J. Davis 126, 217, 226, 235, 237. J.C. Gilham 48, 186. G.L. Gundry 35. G.L. Gundry collection 34. P.T. Hay 177, 197, 198, 229. Alan A. Jackson 2, 3, 4, 5, 6, 7, 8, 9, 10, 16, 18, 20, 21, 22, 25, 33, 36, 38, 41, 51, 53, 56, 68, 71, 72, 74, 84, 86, 88, 90, 95, 98, 114, 115, 124, 128, 130, 132, 135, 150, 151, 153, 154, 157, 161, 162, 165, 176, 187, 188, 189, 211, 213, 220, 268. A.P. & M. Jacobs 138. J.H. Price 63, 65, 209. R.C. Riley 19, 97. H.J. Patterson Rutherford 24, 47, 74, 78, 80, 243, 263. B. Sankey 223. H. Gordon Tidey 119, A.G. Wells 271. G.T. Wheway 11, 12, 13. Author 8, 23, 28, 31, 39, 40, 45, 46, 49, 52, 54, 57, 58, 59, 60, 62, 64, 66, 67, 73, 75, 76, 81, 82, 87, 89, 91, 93, 101, 102, 104, 106, 108, 109, 112, 113, 117, 122, 133, 140, 142, 144, 146, 148, 152, 155, 159, 164, 166, 168, 169, 170, 172, 174, 178, 180, 181, 182, 184, 190, 192, 193, 195, 197, 199, 200, 201, 202, 204, 205, 206, 207, 210, 212, 214, 216, 218, 224, 225, 231, 232, 233, 234, 236, 239, 241, 242, 244, 245, 246, 247, 248, 250, 251, 252, 253, 254, 255, 256, 257, 258, 259, 260, 262, 264, 265, 266, 267, 269, 270. Author's collection 14, 15, 26, 29, 30, 32, 37, 42, 43, 44, 50, 55, 61, 67, 83, 92, 94, 100, 105, 111, 129, 134, 139, 141, 143, 145, 147, 149, 156, 163, 167, 171, 185, 191, 194, 203, 208, 219, 221, 227, 228, 240, 272.

The main source for the text was the photographs. However, the historical details depend on a large number of documentary sources. It is perhaps invidious to select particular works for mention, as the basis is merely the extent to which they were consulted. Locomotive details come mainly from the definitive works published by the Railway Correspondence and Travel Society – *Locomotives of the GWR*, *Locomotives of the LNER* and *Locomotives of the Southern Railway*. In addition information was obtained from the RCTS *Locomotive Stock Books* covering the period 1934 to 1976 and the *Coaching Stock of British Railways*, 1976.

Closure dates come mainly from *Clinker's Register*. Opening dates were taken from numerous sources, including *Bradshaw's Guide* and the various company histories, of which George Dow's *Great Central* is an excellent example. Ownership was ascertained by reference to the Railway Clearing House official publications, especially the *Junction Diagrams*. Other details came from official *Working Timetables*. In addition to books, articles in periodicals proved most helpful, especially the earlier accounts from the *Railway Magazine*.

Personal help, like the documentary references, merits a longer list than space permits. However, I should, particularly like to mention Bill Waller, of B.T. Batsford, who waited patiently, and finally saw the work through the press, and Sandra Chivers, who converted my almost indecipherable writing into an acceptable typescript. My friend Alan A. Jackson examined the typescript and made many helpful suggestions. My wife was patient and tolerant over my protracted pre-occupation with the subject of this book. I would also like to thank the National Railway Museum and the staff of British Rail for their contribution. Finally, may I apologise to all the writers and informants that I have not specifically mentioned – I have not forgotten my debt to them.

Introduction

The concept of a special bearing surface to facilitate the passage of people and goods is an ancient one. The advantage of wheels running on rails was probably first exploited in the mines of Central Europe in the medieval period. In Britain three main phases of railway history may be distinguished, each with subdivisions: the horse railway period, from about 1600 to about 1830, followed by the steam railway, which was replaced by the modern railway in the 1960s. Clearly this is a simplification. For instance, a horse railway, such as the Merchant's Railway on Portland, lasted until 1939, and many of the characteristics of steam railways are still to be seen in the 1970s. Nevertheless, the 1830s and the 1960s were revolutionary periods.

The present work is not a scientific examination of the railways in the 1960s, but aims rather to record some of the visual changes that took place. The technological, social and economic reasons for these changes are implied but not stated. For instance, the date of closure of a branch line is given without a detailed analysis of the reasons that brought about this particular closure. The changing scene is described in a series of short essays on particular views.

The first revolution, from horse to steam traction, from mainly mineral to general traffic, from tracks laid out for low speeds to tracks laid out for higher speeds, receives some attention. Track on stone blocks at St Keyne (240) or horses at work (271) both show horse railway scenes in the steam railway period. However, attention is concentrated on the change from steam to modern railways, including changes in the track, in the buildings, in rolling stock and in techniques of traffic control.

The Railway

Typical track of the steam period consisted of bull-head steel rail, fixed in chairs and supported and held to gauge by wooden sleepers. This type of rail, and the flat-bottomed track which succeeded it, is shown at Harringay (7), while the continuous welded rail of the modern railway is shown at New Malden (36). Examples of chairs from various companies are illustrated (243–8). Points were operated mechanically with point rodding, as at Southend (118). A view at Enfield shows points operated from a ground frame, with a facing point lock, as required for passenger lines, and others worked by a spring lever, on an adjacent siding (3). Before the advent of electrical track circuits, trains literally made their presence felt by fouling bars, as at Swanley Junction (70). On modern railways, points are operated by electric point motors, illustrated at St Pancras (10). The elaborate hydraulic buffers, once a feature of terminal stations, have almost gone, but simple buffer stops, as shown at Preston (188), are easily found. With the advent of double-ended electric and diesel locomotives, turntables have become a thing of the past. The closure of many goods depots has combined with such developments as set trains and longer wagons to bring about the elimination of wagon turntables, as viewed at Exeter (242).

In some cases, power for moving the trains was taken from the line, as with atmospheric railways, rope-worked inclines and electrification. Inclines at Cowlairs (228), Werneth (198) and Hopton (177) are illustrated, while examples of both live rail and overhead wires are recorded at Tulse Hill (17) and Euston (11–13). Lineside feeder cables are shown at North Acton (33). The need for protective fencing has increased with higher train speeds and electrification. A number of types of barrier are illustrated, including stone walls at Sudbrook (217) and Cowlairs (228), wire with wooden posts at Shawford (55) and, rather exceptionally, metal at Rye (92). During the steam period it was common practice to permit railwaymen to cultivate allotments inside the fence. In addition, when many more horses were in use on the roads and railways, it was usual to harvest a hay crop from the lineside. A hay rick is shown at Yarmouth in the Isle of Wight (47).

When railways were first constructed, interference with the established road network was usually avoided by means of bridges. However, at points where the railway was neither in a cutting or on an embankment, gated level crossings were sometimes permitted. On modern railways, they are either replaced by bridges, or else automatic or remotely controlled lifting barriers are substituted for gates. Level crossings illustrated include Purfleet (121–2), White Notley (105–6) and Southampton (63–4). Acceptable gradients were achieved by earthworks and the provision of tunnels and viaducts, and water was crossed by bridges. These have not changed as much as the less durable elements in the railway scene. Nevertheless, wooden viaducts, of the type in use near Witham (99) are virtually extinct. Examples of tunnel replacement, such as that at Woodhead (202–4), are rare. Iron bridges were usually replaced by steel during the steam period; one example is Sutton Bridge (183–4).

Buildings

Railway buildings may be placed in three main categories – stations (i.e. passenger terminals), goods depots (i.e. freight terminals) and service buildings such as platelayer's huts or engine sheds. All three categories have been affected by the recent changes. Station facilities have been reduced, and in many cases buildings which included booking offices, waiting rooms, conveniences and a station master's house have been replaced by simple shelters similar to those provided at bus stops. Horse railways rarely carried passengers, but elaborate passenger stations, sometimes handling little traffic, were a feature of the steam railways. An outstanding example is the magnificent building at Maldon (100–2), now preserved as a restaurant. However, modest buildings of wood or, more exceptionally, of corrugated iron, were by no means unknown in the steam period, as at Sheerness-on-Sea (74) or Rye (92). A characteristic feature of British railways was the provision of a platform to assist passengers getting in and out of trains. In the steam period these were sometimes wooden. Wood was particularly favoured for sites on embankments; elsewhere a brick, stone or concrete face, with a gravel, blacktop or stone surface was normal. Examples shown include Crewe (187) with a stone surface. Where platforms were low, either steps were provided on

coaches, or portable steps, resembling a mounting block, were kept on platforms – for example Woody Bay (163) and Three Cocks (215).

In addition to being assisted by platforms, passengers were protected from the weather by awnings. These usually projected from the buildings, as at Hythe (80), and were sometimes carried over the track to protect both passengers and rolling stock, as for example at St Albans (127). Major terminals had most impressive overall roofs, such as Cannon Street (19). The tendency has been to replace overall roofs with platform awnings, as at Barbican (27–8) or to dispense with them altogether, an example being St Albans (128). At many stations facilities went beyond the issue of tickets and the provision of waiting accommodation and shelter. For instance, refreshment rooms were opened – Three Cocks (215) – bookstalls were erected, – Bognor (94) – and automatic machines installed – Shanklin (265). Seats were placed on the platforms, as at Lewisham (252). Lighting was provided, usually with oil lamps in the country – Christow (143) or Colyford (160) – and gas in the towns – Bath (165). The modern equivalent is electric strip lighting, as shown at Fenchurch Street (2). Stations have been identified by station nameboards – Hastings (85) – by names on lights – Crewe (187) – and by names on seats – Canning Town (253). For many years access to station yards was controlled, and only privileged cabs were allowed to stand on railway property. Yards are no longer gated, in the way shown at Maldon (100), although comparison may be made with the barriers installed at some station car parks.

The most striking change in goods depots is the number of closures. In the steam period most passenger stations were combined with goods depots, but this is no longer the case. Typical examples, with transit sheds for goods traffic are shown at Prestonpans (225) and Heathfield (90). At Chalford (141) there were no buildings for freight, it being quite normal to transfer direct from rail to road vehicles or, in the case of less perishable traffic such as coal or building materials, to a nearby storage point. Modern railways depend on a limited number of depots with a high throughput. Freightliner depots are a new development but private sidings, after numerous closures – such as Forres (236) – are now being revived.

In addition to buildings associated with traffic there have been numerous buildings used in connection with the maintenance of railway services. Perhaps the best known are the motive power depots, which, with the end of steam, have undergone both a reduction of numbers and a change of character. Major steam depots are shown at Norwich (109) and Crewe (186). Smaller sheds appear at Enfield (3) and Rye (92). The view at Machynlleth (213–14) shows the conversion of a depot from steam to diesel. The familiar coaling stages and watering points have some relationship to oil fueling points – Norwich (109). Platelayers' huts were often built of wood, but the example at Shawford Junction (56) is of concrete. During the steam period when, especially in urban areas, a combination of semaphore signals and fog could make things very difficult for drivers, permanent way staff were posted at distant signals to place detonators on the line to give a warning if the signal was on. They were provided with small huts resembling sentry boxes, as at Norwich (110). For general mess rooms it was not unusual to provide old coach bodies, as shown at Stoke Ferry (111). On modern railways fogmen are rarely called out and platelayers often use their road vehicles as mess rooms, so there has been a notable decline in the number of fogmans' and platelayers' huts.

One of the most characteristic buildings of the steam period railway was the signal box. Some were built by signal manufacturers, but most were built to the requirements of the owning company. Thus, it was possible to distinguish a Midland Railway Box – St Pancras (9) – a South Eastern – Knockholt (263) – or a London & South Western – Axminster (158). With mechanical operating there were limits on the distance over which points and semaphore signals could be operated, and numerous boxes were required. With power operating there are virtually no limits, and modern signalling schemes cover considerable areas from one centre. Signal boxes were frequently sited at stations and, with their semaphore signals, the total number of oil lamps in use would be considerable. Because of the smell and fire danger it was usual to provide separate huts, constructed of corrugated iron, where lamps could be filled with parafin oil.

Rolling Stock

To produce transport the railway must be equipped with suitable rolling stock, and the change in this respect has hardly been less than that in the buildings. Rolling stock is considered under three main heads. First, separate power units, such as steam, electric or diesel locomotives, and horses; second, combined power and carrying units – for example, electric motor coaches; and thirdly, hauled stock, including passenger coaches and freight wagons. In addition, brief notice is taken of stock not on the rails but associated with the railways, such as horse drawn hotel buses, based on stations.

The railways were major users of horses, not only during the horse railway period but also in the steam era, both for shunting and cartage services. In the latter period horse traction of passenger vehicles was confined to local lines, the last example in England being the Port Carlisle branch of the North British Railway, converted to steam in 1914. The examples shown are on independent lines, the Fairbourne (219) and Southend Pier (129). A horse railway at Portland is shown (149) and shunting on a steam railway is illustrated at Whitstable (271).

Clearly all forms of motive power, including horses, are at their best on particular duties, but in the case of steam locomotives there were very obvious adaptions. For instance, the time and distance away from coaling and watering facilities was the deciding factor in whether a locomotive had a separate tender, or whether water and coal supplies were carried on the same frame. Wheel diameter, acting as a rough equivalent to gearing, indicated whether a locomotive was mainly for lighter and faster passenger work, or slower and heavier freight. Steam locomotives for express passenger work had tenders, and wheels of larger diameter. Examples from the pre-grouping period are shown from the SECR at Knockholt (263) and the GWR at Dawlish (139). The 1923 grouping reduced the variety of types of locomotives, but the period between the wars probably saw the highest development of the steam locomotive. Express locomotives from this period are shown in a number of views including Cannon Street (19) and St Pancras (9). Some of the Southern Railway's express locomotives were rebuilt by British Railways, as shown at Shawford Junction (56) and Axminster (158). For short distance work tank locomotives were used, and if there was a less continuous demand for a high power output, a smaller boiler was provided. A number of examples are shown. From the pre-grouping period, of especial interest are the locomotives seen at New Malden (34), Manchester (196),

Highbridge (131) and Ongar (96). Tank locomotives built between the wars are shown at Verney Junction (175), Enfield (4) and Barbican (27). British Railways designs are shown at Barking (115) and Purfleet (121). Freight locomotives were usually provided with tenders, but shunting was normally carried out by tank locomotives. A typical freight locomotive is shown at Exeter (136) and a locomotive engaged in shunting passenger coaches is shown at Norwich (110).

One of the most important changes of the 1960s was the final elimination of steam traction from the standard gauge lines of British Railways. Most of the electric locomotives were built to take current from overhead wires, but the Southern Region had a design equipped for collection from a live rail. The majority of the electric locomotives used on hauled stock were concentrated on the London Midland Region, as shown at Euston (13) and Cheddington (172). A Southern Region locomotive is illustrated at Dover (79). Diesel locomotives were rather more varied in design. Most of them used an electric power transmission system. Typical examples are shown at St Pancras (10), Norwich (110), Crewe (187), Wareham (155) and Dawlish (140). Diesel hydraulic locomotives were confined to the Western Region, and one of them is shown at Norton Fitzwarren (135). Diesel shunters were markedly different in appearance, perhaps the most obvious distinction being that they only had one cab.

The idea of combining a coach and motive power unit on the same frame was developed, after some earlier experiments, during the Edwardian period. A steam rail motor car is shown at Chalford on the GWR (141). The SECR operated steam cars, and although the locomotive sections were abandoned, the coaches were still in use at Leysdown in 1950 (76). Because electric traction equipment could be put into less space than steam, it was convenient to combine it with coaches. Ease of remote control made it possible to place powered coaches at different positions in a train, all driven from one cab. For express services locomotives are normal, but the Southern Region operates express multiple units consisting of permanently coupled sets of powered cars and trailers. Examples are shown at Woking (39) and Southampton (69). For short distance services, with more frequent reversals in terminals, multiple-unit operation is virtually universal. The London Transport fleet consists almost entirely of such trains, and examples for operation in tube tunnels are shown at North Acton Junction (32–3) and Ongar (98). Similar coaches now in use on the Isle of Wight are illustrated at Sandown (51). Multiple-unit stock of an independent railway is shown on Southend Pier (130), and of British Railways at Enfield (5) and at Barking (117). Diesel motors can be distributed along a train, and can be remotely controlled in the same way as electric motors. Any number of cars can form a train, such as the one car shown at Verney Junction (176) or six cars, as photographed at Harringay (8). The Southern went in for electric transmission, and a diesel electric multiple unit is shown at Three Bridges (86).

Because they work over both electrified and non-electrified lines, but especially because they spend less time in motion, freight wagons and vans are not self-propelled. They have undergone as much change as anything else, from small wagons with only a handbrake (many of them privately owned) to modern wagons designed for particular traffics and with continuous brakes. Photographs including typical steam period wagons were taken at Newport (269) and Whitstable (271). Modern Freightliner wagons are shown at Eastleigh (59). Passenger coaches have also changed considerably, the compartment coach, once standard for local journeys, now being rare. Compartment coaches are illustrated at Highbridge (131), Werneth (198) and Verney Junction (175). Main line coaches of various types appear in a number of views, including Crewe (186–7), Dover (78–9) and Axminster (158–9).

Rolling stock associated with the railways, but not on rails, has also changed. For example, platform trolleys, usually with electric or manual traction, have altered considerably. The traditional type, such as that seen at Manchester (196), has been replaced by the British Railways Utility Trolley – 'Brute' – as photographed at Bognor (95). Attempts have been made to co-ordinate road and rail transport with motor buses and taxis outside stations. However, the degree of co-ordination is often rather less than that of the Edwardian period, with its horse drawn carriages and buses to be found in many station yards, as shown at Maldon (100). Railway vans and carts have been mechanised for many years, but a horse-drawn example is at Ashtead (272). Any one of these changes is worth detailed study, but the photographs indicated will give a definite impression of the sort of changes that have occurred.

Traffic Control

Traffic on horse railways was sufficiently light and slow to minimize the need for train control. However, as they normally consisted of single lines with passing places, it was usual to formulate rules governing precedence for trains that met in between. Either the traffic in one direction had the right of way, or the train nearest a passing place had to return to it. Posts indicated the half way point. With faster and heavier steam trains double track solved the problem of head on collisions, but visual signals were provided to avoid collisions at junctions, or between trains travelling on the same line. An early form of signal consisted of a disc and crossbar, swivelling to indicate whether or not the track ahead was clear. An example is shown at Dawlish (138). Eventually (perhaps due to the influence of former naval officers serving on the railways) semaphore signals were introduced and came to control virtually all the traffic on running lines. Although signals were sometimes purchased from outside manufacturers, most of the large companies had their own distinctive designs. As an example, two typical Midland signals on a bracketed post are illustrated at Upminster (123). Between the wars three out of the four main companies substituted arms working in the upper quadrant for those working in the lower, and a Midland bracketed post with LMS upper quadrant arms is shown at St Pancras (9). The LNW favoured tall wooden posts in positions at which overbridges obstructed vision, with co-acting arms visible over or under the bridge, as exemplified at Cheddington (172). A similar arrangement from the LCDR is illustrated at Swanley Junction (70) but with a metal lattice post. The GW retained the lower quadrant arm, and a GWR speciality was a centre balance arm for use in restricted space, as at Highbridge (132). Another unusual design was the somersault arm, particularly associated with the GNR, although the example shown was on the M & GN at Sutton Bridge (183). Where signals were provided for a number of tracks, especially at the approaches to junctions, they were frequently mounted on gantries. Examples shown include Barking (114) with both upper and lower quadrant arms, and Northam, Southampton (62).

From early days railways continued to operate in darkness, and signals were provided with lamps which showed up at night to indicate the position of the arms. On underground lines, in permanent darkness, arms were not provided. Semaphores survived with oil lamps because there were difficulties in obtaining a light of sufficient intensity to show against bright sunshine, but with electricity this was no longer difficult. The colour light signal proved effective by day and night, and also in fog, and could be remotely or automatically controlled rather more easily than a semaphore. Colour lights form part of the modern railway scene and, as they are constructed by outside manufacturers, do not show regional variations. Examples illustrated include signals from St Johns (25–6) showing junction indications, New Malden (35) and St Pancras (10).

In addition to controlling traffic on running lines, shunting and other incidental movements must be regulated, and distinctive signals are provided for this purpose. When they are directed at stationary or slow moving trains they are often placed near the ground, and described as ground signals. An illustration is given from Lincoln (182). Semaphore signals were normally operated by means of wires from lever frames in strategically placed signal cabins. These appear on many of the views, including Morfa Mawddach (211). Although the lever frames were usually placed in cabins, there were exceptions. In particular, small frames were sometimes placed at ground level, without protection, as shown at Enfield (3). Modern railways have large numbers of automatic signals, and both the semaphore signal and the instruments and lever frames with which it was associated are becoming rare.

The equipment described above covers track occupation and traffic control, but other types of information are provided for drivers. For instance, at stations served by multiple-unit trains there is usually an indication of the points at which a driver should stop, depending on the number of coaches in his train. For example, the stopping point for 10 coach trains is shown at St Johns (25–6), and for 6 or 8 coach trains at New Malden (35). Permanent speed restriction signs are shown at Morfa Mawddach (211) and Exeter (137). While not strictly part of traffic regulation, information about the running of trains is provided by train control. This may be visual, as shown by the Next Train indicator at Barbican (27), or verbal, as indicated by the provision of loud speakers at Three Bridges (86). An essential element for traffic regulation was communication, and from the 1840s, this was provided by the electric telegraph, supplemented later by the telephone. Modern railways place the wires in a protected position, underground, but in the steam railway period they were carried on the tall poles which feature in a number of views, including Norton Fitzwarren (135) and Cheddington (171). Also in the steam period, individual loading of wagons took place in numerous depots, and it was necessary to check that the appropriate height and width was not exceeded. Loading gauges were provided at most depots, as shown at Chalford (141) and Chatham (72), but are now rare.

Miscellaneous

A number of aspects of the railways scene do not fit obviously into the four sections which have been described. For instance, information about the line is provided by mile posts and gradient posts. Mile posts are shown at Hythe (80) and Stanhope (241), and gradient posts at Sutton Bridge (183) and Hopton (177). Railway companies indicated the extent of their land ownership by boundary marks, as illustrated at Swansea (258), Stratford (257) and

Gravesend (259). Further, they posted warnings, made in iron, to potential trespassers. The examples shown include warnings from Pontyates (255) and Blaenau Festiniog (210). Pre-grouping companies maintained poster boards on stations and other property frequented by the public, as illustrated at Sheerness (74) and Yarmouth, Isle of Wight (47).

Water was required in considerable quantities for steam locomotives and in moderate quantities for other uses. At points where demand was considerable, large elevated tanks were provided, and replenished by hand, wind or steam operated pumps. A number of these are illustrated, including Three Bridges (86) and Axminster (158). Locomotives took water from water cranes, as shown at Southampton (68) and Chatham (72). Gas was used for lighting of both stations and coaches, and also for cooking on restaurant cars. Gas lighting is shown on many of the stations, including New Malden (34). Points for charging coaches with gas are shown at Oxford (266). Railway gas works have gone with the steam era, and water tanks are becoming increasingly rare.

The views that follow comprise an attempt to indicate ways in which the railway scene has changed with the transition from the steam to the modern railway.

14

GWR Great Western Railway

LMSR London Midland & Scottish Railway

Constituents:

England

LNWR	London & North Western Railway
LYR	Lancashire & Yorkshire Railway
MR	Midland Railway (LTSR London Tilbury & Southend Railway)

Scotland

CR	Caledonian Railway
GSWR	Glasgow & South Western Railway
HR	Highland Railway

LNER London & North Eastern Railway

Constituents:

England

GCR	Great Central Railway (MSLR Manchester, Sheffield and Lincolnshire Railway)
GER	Great Eastern Railway (ECR Eastern Counties Railway)
GNR	Great Northern Railway
NER	North Eastern Railway (SDR Stockton & Darlington Railway)

Scotland

GNSR	Great North of Scotland Railway
NBR	North British Railway

SR Southern Railway

Constituents:

Mainland

LSWR	London & South Western Railway
LBSCR	London, Brighton and South Coast Railway
SER	South Eastern Railway
LCDR	London Chatham & Dover Railway
SECR	South Eastern and Chatham Joint Managing Committee

Isle of Wight

FYNR	Freshwater, Yarmouth and Newport Railway
IWCR	Isle of Wight Central Railway
IWR	Isle of Wight Railway

*   *   *

Joint Lines

MGNJR	Midland & Great Northern Railway
SDJR	Somerset and Dorset Joint Railway

Societies

LCGB	Locomotive Club of Great Britain
RCTS	Railway Correspondence and Travel Society

1 London and Middlesex

1, 2 Fenchurch Street, formerly Great Eastern Railway (TQ 334808), on 22 August 1926 and 23 March 1963

Fenchurch Street was opened as the terminus of the London and Blackwall Railway when it was extended from the Minories in 1841. The present building was completed in 1854. Fenchurch Street was connected to the Eastern Counties Railway (later GER) in 1849 and became the London terminus for the trains of the London, Tilbury and Southend Railway in 1854. It became part of the London and North Eastern Railway in 1923 and was transferred to British Railways, Eastern Region, in 1949.

The photograph of 1926 was taken from platform 4, which was used exclusively by LMS (formerly LTS) trains. LMS No.2116, standing on the release road, was a 4-4-2 tank locomotive of LTS design, constructed at Derby in 1923 and scrapped in 1951. The destination board is marked Southend. The short platform 1 (left) was used by the Blackwall trains until they were withdrawn in 1926. Platform 5, which is off the photograph, was used by the North Woolwich trains, and 2 and 3 by other LNER trains, typical destinations being Ilford and Ongar. LNE No.7106 was a 2-4-2 tank locomotive, the LNER classification being F4, constructed at Stratford in 1905 and scrapped in 1933. The destination board is marked Woolwich, and it bears the appropriate discs forming the head code. In 1926 Fenchurch Street was signalled mechanically, and point rodding, semaphore signals and ground signals are visible. The semaphores of GER origin in the centre of the photograph had the following functions, reading from left

to right: plat. 2 Down Slow; plat. 2 Down Fast (upper); plat. 2 to Siding (lower); plat. 3 to Down Slow; plat. 3 to Down Fast (upper); plat. 3 to Siding (lower). Between 1933 and 1935, the platforms were replaced by two island platforms, one for LNE traffic and one for the LMS. The numbering of the platforms was changed from 1 to 5 to 1 to 4, and at the same time a new signal box with power operating was constructed.

The photograph of 1963 was taken from platform 2, formerly the LNE platform. This was provided with overhead electric wires in 1949 when the electric service from Liverpool Street to Shenfield was inaugurated, but there was no public electric service to Fenchurch Street. All platforms were provided with overhead wires by 1961, when electric services on the former LTS began. The photograph shows No.248, a 4-car set of Class 302, constructed partly at York and partly at Doncaster Works in 1959. It is bound for Shoeburyness and carries the LTS line headcode 2132. Electrification with multiple-unit stock made simplification of the track layout possible, and platform 1/2 was extended to approximately the same length as 3/4. The original overall roof remained, which, with a span of 101 feet and a length of 300 feet, must protect a smaller proportion of the coaches of trains than any other comparable terminal roof. Fenchurch Street remains essentially a London area station, having as its longest journey the $39\frac{1}{2}$ miles to Shoeburyness.

3, 4, 5 Enfield Town, formerly Great Eastern Railway (TQ 329966), on 9 March 1957, 13 September 1958 and 19 June 1965

The branch from the Northern and Eastern Railway (later GER) in the Lea Valley to Enfield was opened in 1849. The rapid growth of the town led to the construction of a new station in 1872, and this survived, with minor changes, until 1957. The photograph taken in that year shows the brick-faced platform sheltered by a long canopy with an ornate valance. The ground frame operates the turnout for an engine release road, which is fully protected with a fouling bar and a lock. In contrast, the points on the right, not being on a track carrying passenger trains, are operated simply by a spring-loaded lever. In the distance the motive power depot is visible; these depots were provided at many of the outer suburban terminals. The trolley on the platform is piled high with mail bags and on the far side of the platform typical LNER compartment stock is visible.

By 1958, there are signs of the rebuilding of the station. The platform road has been slewed to roughly the position of the former release road and the platform face, now made of concrete blocks, has been moved over to reach it. The ground frame has been moved to a new position alongside the brick retaining wall. This allowed for releasing locomotives from the shed via the platform road, but, as there was now direct access from the shed road, a trap had been inserted in the track leading from the engine shed. The train consists of one of the 4-coach articulated sets, built by the LNER for the former GE services. It was hauled by an 0-6-2 tank locomotive of the N7/5 class, No.69665, based on Shed 30A (Stratford). This was constructed by R. Stephenson & Co. in 1925 and scrapped in 1960.

Electric services were introduced in November 1960, by which time the rebuilding of the station had been completed. The photograph of 1965 shows that the basic design of one island and one single faced platform was retained, but the island platform had been widened and given a new roof and new platform furniture. The engine shed was closed in November 1960 and a low platform to assist carriage cleaners was provided on the site. Set 439, a 3 car set of Class 305/1 constructed at York in 1960, appears to have the letter missing from its headcode. The provision of overhead live wires and resignalling completed the transformation of Enfield.

---

6 King's Cross Station, formerly Great Northern Railway (TQ 303830), on 17 September 1958

At King's Cross dieselisation of motive power was not accompanied by new signalling or re-arrangement of tracks. (This did not take place until 1977.) This view records the transition from steam to diesel motive power, with A1 class 4-6-2 No.60130 based on Shed 56C (Copley Hill) having arrived on the up Yorkshire Pullman at the platform then numbered 4. No.60130, named 'Kestrel', was constructed at Darlington Works in 1948 and scrapped in 1965. Refinements such as smoke deflectors, the generator for electric lamps and the automatic warning equipment are visible. Accessories of steam include the water crane with its drainage arrangements and the ashes visible on the track. Alongside, No.D208, later allocated to Class 40 and re-numbered 40008, is ready to leave as a light engine, with rear lamp in position. It was completed at the Vulcan Foundry in 1958. The outline of the magnificent roof, 800 ft long and 105 ft wide, has not changed since the opening of the station in 1852, although the wooden ribs were replaced by metal in 1869–70.

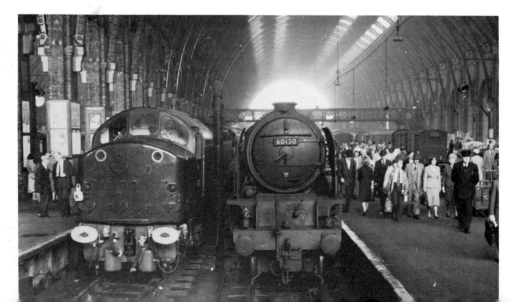

7, 8 Harringay Station, formerly Great Northern Railway (TQ 314882), on 2 July 1955 and 2 July 1976

Harringay was constructed on the GN main line to serve a growing residential area in 1885. It was sited at a point where the line skirts a hill, and successive widenings of the line necessitated the securing of a greater width by excavating the hill side, and securing it with a retaining wall. The wooden station buildings were situated on a footbridge. The view of 1955 shows an express running through the station on the up main line, hauled by A1 class 4-6-2 No.60119. This was named 'Patrick Stirling' and was constructed at Doncaster Works in 1948 and scrapped in 1964. At this time both chaired and flat-bottomed rails were in use. The bridge in the background carried the flyover from the up side to Hornsey Carriage Sidings.

By 1973 the bridge had been replaced, and work had begun on the provision of new station buildings on the footbridge. Alterations at platform level included the replacement of the waiting rooms and the reduction of the number of platform faces from four to two. Re-alignment and change of use of the tracks, together with the provision of coloured light signals, was complete when the second photograph was taken, exactly 11 years after the first. At this time overhead electric wires were in position, but electric trains did not begin running until November 1976. The multiple-unit diesel set approaching Harringay was forming the 18.26 departure for the York Road platform at King's Cross, running on the up local line (formerly the down main).

9, 10 St Pancras Station, formerly Midland Railway (TQ 302830), on 7 May 1955 and 2 November 1963

St Pancras Station was opened as the prestigious London terminal of the Midland Railway in 1868. The main building has undergone less change than almost any other main station, but the two photographs record changes in signalling and motive power. The 1955 view shows a double headed express, with Jubilee class No.45594 'Bhopal' as the train engine, about to leave from platform 5. This locomotive was constructed by the North British Locomotive Co. in 1935 and withdrawn in 1962. Three phrases of semaphore signalling are visible. On the left, the Midland Railway gantry retains its lower quadrant semaphore arms. In the centre, an asymmetrical bracket signal retains its original posts, with characteristic MR finials, but has been provided with LMS upper quadrant arms. These form the starter signals for platforms 3 and 4; the starter for platform 5 consists of a

tubular metal post with upper quadrant arm. The signal cabin is typically Midland, constructed of wood with a hipped roof, a gallery and a row of fire buckets. In front of the signal box is the hydraulically operated lift for transferring wagons to a lower level. One of the hydraulic capstans, used for moving the wagons, is visible.

Although partly obscured by the locomotive and the electric distribution boxes in the photograph, the lift was still *in situ* in 1963. The diesel locomotive, D123, was constructed at Crewe Works in 1961. It was allocated to Class 45 and re-numbered 45125. The power signal box had been opened in 1957 alongside the line to the left of the picture. Both power-operated points and colour light signals are visible. The next phase of development at St Pancras will be the provision of overhead electric wires.

11, 12, 13 Euston Station, formerly London and North Western Railway (TQ 295828), on 3 October 1962, 30 April 1964 and 31 August 1968

Euston is one of London's oldest terminals, opened on the London and Birmingham Railway in 1837. Conversely it is the most modern, having undergone more radical rebuilding than any other London terminal. The three photographs record re-building on the east side, with three views from platform 3. In 1962 it was still possible to trace the evolution of the station. Platform 3 marked the site of the original arrival platform and platform 6 indicated the position of the departure platform. In the early 1870s an additional platform, later numbered 1/2, was added beyond the arrival platform, and the lighting was improved and smoke dispersal facilitated by raising the roof of the train shed by six feet. It remained, however, lower than the arched roofs of the newer neighbouring terminals of St Pancras and King's Cross. The positions of the columns supporting the roof, visible in the photograph between the platforms, were not changed, and coaches continued to reach the sidings between the platforms by means of traversers, which passed through gaps in the line of columns. Because of this, no LNW coaches exceeded 33 feet in length until after 1882. In 1891 the carriage sidings were replaced by a wooden island platform, which was later numbered 4/5. The view also shows platforms added to the west of the original station. Seven was a bay at the end of No.6, while the train sheds beyond, added in about 1840, covered platforms 8, 9 and 10 (10 was not used for passenger traffic). In 1952 the main arrival and departure platforms were

lengthened, and a new signal box with power-operated points and colour light signals was opened. One of the electro-pneumatic point motors is visible in the foreground of the photograph. In 1962 trains were being moved by steam, diesel or electric power, and evidence of two of these forms of power appears on the photograph. Live rails were provided for platforms 4, 5 and 7 in 1922 for the electric service to Watford. Evidence of steam is provided by the water crane on the end of Platform 6.

The photograph of 1964 shows transformation in an advanced stage, and that of 1968 shows it completed. By 1964 the platforms were either new or rebuilt, and concrete replaced either brick and stone or timber. Demolition was still in progress on the sites of platforms 8 to 10, but the construction stage had been reached on the site of platforms 3 to 7. The view of 1968 shows the new Euston. Live rails have gone from this part of the station, but overhead electric wires have been installed. Electric power reigns, and three main line electric locomotives are shown. The coaches are all of the BR Mk2 variety and even the traditional hand trolleys, still in evidence in 1964, have been replaced by the more flexible 'Brutes'. Modern electric lighting is installed, which revives the traditional railway device of showing the name of the station on the lamp glass. The signals are new, and there are no clear survivals from 1962 on the photographs of 1968.

14, 15, 16 Gunnersbury Station, formerly London and South Western Railway (TQ 198784), in about 1906, in 1950 and on 22 February 1975

From an historical viewpoint Gunnersbury is one of the most interesting stations on the suburban system of the LSWR, having been served at various times by trains of six companies – Great Western, London and South Western, Metropolitan, Metropolitan District, Midland and North London. It was opened on the LSW line from Addison Road, Kensington to Richmond in 1869 as Brentford Road. To the south of the station a line diverged to join the LSW Hounslow loop, and to the north there was a connection to the North and South Western Junction line at South Acton. The latter was owned jointly by the LNWR, Midland and North London companies and was used by Midland and North London trains serving Richmond. The GW, Metropolitan and Metropolitan District trains for Richmond all joined the LSW in Hammersmith, the Metropolitan and GW at Grove Road Junction and the District at Studland Road Junction. South of Gunnersbury, all trains went to Richmond, except for the LSW service to Twickenham via the Hounslow loop.

In the first view, taken in about 1906 from the south end of the station, the scene is typical of the LSWR except for the live rails provided for the District trains. Particularly characteristic are the signals and the station canopies. The lines serving Richmond and the Hounslow loop, those to the North London line via the N & SW Junction, and to Waterloo via Kensington, all connected north of the station. Because of this there were two routes through the station, that to the Hounslow loop being on the west side (to the left on the photograph), and that to Richmond on the east side. To Richmond there were two down tracks and one up, but although all three were electrified for the District trains in 1905, only two show signs of use for electric services. The bracket signal serves the two down Richmond tracks, and the arrangement of arms indicates that trains using the platform on which the train is standing could be signalled for either the Hounslow loop or Richmond. In fact, as a signal has been pulled off for an up North London train, it is possible that the train held at the platform was destined for the Hounslow loop. The station buildings are typical of the 1860s on the LSWR, and are visible at the top of the cutting on the left hand side.

By 1950, there has been a number of developments. The station was owned and operated by the Southern Region of British Railways, as successors to the LSWR, but train services were provided, to quote a notice on the canopy over the station entrance, by 'London Transport and LM Region Electric Trains'. These were the successors of the Metropolitan District and the North London Railway trains, the former being electrically operated from 1905 and the latter from 1916. Of the LSW services, that to the Hounslow loop had been withdrawn in 1915, and the Waterloo to Richmond service via Kensington and Hammersmith at the end of 1916. In 1932 the spur to the Hounslow loop was abandoned together with the platforms on either side of the station, all traffic being concentrated on the western of the two island platforms. The surviving buildings are unchanged, but the upper quadrant arm of the down starting signal is typical of the Southern Railway.

The final view, taken in 1975 from almost the same viewpoint, illustrates Gunnersbury after the changes which took place in 1964. In connection with a major development scheme, the buildings were demolished and all of the station site not in railway use was built upon. The semaphore signal has been replaced by a colour light and there have been alterations to the platform. Appropriately enough the platform is occupied by an LT Richmond Train, a successor to the Metropolitan District steam trains which began to call at Gunnersbury in 1877.

17, 18 Tulse Hill Station, formerly London, Brighton and South Coast Railway (TQ 318 729), on 17 March 1928 and 13 July 1957

Tulse Hill has a certain amount in common with Gunnersbury. It was opened on the LBSCR line from Peckham to Sutton in 1868, with connecting spurs onto the earlier line between Victoria, Balham and Crystal Palace at the country end of the station being added in 1870 and 1871. In 1869 a connection at the London end led to the London, Chatham and Dover main line at Herne Hill. This made possible the service from the LCD City stations to Wimbledon via Streatham, perpetuated at present by the Holborn Viaduct to London Bridge (via Wimbledon and Sutton) trains.

The LBSC route from London Bridge was electrified on the 6700V 25 cycle system in 1912. The 1928 photograph was taken from the south side of the station and shows the ornate entrance to Knights Hill Tunnel. The train of 6-wheel LBSC compartment coaches is leaving for London Bridge hauled by 0-6-2 tank locomotive No.B490 (later renumbered 2490). This belonged to the LBSC E4 class, was constructed at Brighton Works in 1889 and withdrawn in 1955. Overhead electric trains were still

operating, but the third rail which replaced the overhead wire in June 1928 was already in position. The lower quadrant signals were placed on the gantry supporting the overhead wires, so that the gantry was retained for supporting signals after conversion to third-rail power supply. A disused LBSC signal post is visible in the distance.

When a view was taken from the same platform in 1957, all the gantries had been removed except for that supporting the signal. (The upright is visible at the end of the platform.) The layout had not changed, but on the London Bridge line flat bottomed had replaced chaired rails. The steel underbridge remained, with longitudinal sleepers laid on the metal deck. The train approaching from the Herne Hill direction consists of the empty stock of a train from the Kent Coast, working from Cannon Street via Metropolitan Junction to Eardley Carriage Sidings. The LMR type 2-6-2 tank locomotive is hauling a mixture of Bulleid and Maunsell coaches, some in green and some in 'plum and spilt milk' livery.

19, 20 Cannon Street, formerly South Eastern Railway (TQ 326808), in May 1958 and June 1959

This was the City terminus of the South Eastern Railway, reached by crossing the River Thames from London Bridge. It was constructed at great expense and opened in 1866, one of the few stations within the boundary of the City of London. For many years, the principal SE trains started from the West End terminus at Charing Cross, and ran in and out of Cannon Street before leaving London.

After the First World War this became exceptional, and main line services to Cannon Street were confined to the peak periods. As at Charing Cross the value of City land precluded extensions to the station, and the outside walls of 1866 remained in position.

When the line into Cannon Street was electrified in 1926, a new track layout of a most intricate character was provided. Complexities such as double slip points are visible in the 1959 view, and while breaks in the live rail could not be avoided, they were reduced to a minimum. The live rails were protected by wooden guards in the proximity of the platform. But even more impressive than the trackwork in the 1958 view is the magnificent iron overall roof of 1866. With a span of 190 ft and a length of 680 ft, the Cannon Street roof was in the same class as Paddington, King's Cross and St Pancras. It suffered damage from bombs and lost all its glass, but survived in skeletal form until demolition commenced in April 1958. In the photograph taken at that time, the scaffolding of the demolition contractors is visible. The original intention was to remove the outside walls and the end towers, but public protests were sufficient to achieve their preservation. In the 1959 view the former hotel survives at the far end of the platforms, but this was replaced in 1965 by an office block. In fact the new concourse at Cannon Street has as much of a modern atmosphere as Euston.

The two photographs record the last days of steam on the Hastings line and the Kent Coast lines respectively. The 1958 view, taken during the evening rush hour, shows an express leaving for Hastings from platform 6, a Kent Coast express in platform 7, and a diesel train later to form an express to Hastings in platform 8. Curved tunnels of limited width necessitated bans on standard coaches and many classes of locomotives on the Hastings line.

Special coaches were built, classified by the Southern Railway as Restriction 0; the first batch in 1929 and 1930, and the second in 1934. After being refurbished in 1952 and 1953, they remained in use until supplanted by special diesel trains in 1958. The photograph shows Restriction 0 coaches being hauled by Schools class No.30920 'Rugby', which was built at Eastleigh in 1933 and withdrawn in 1961. Light Pacific No.34021 'Dartmoor' had been rebuilt in January 1958, and is blowing off steam, ready to leave with British Railway Mk 1 coaches for the Kent Coast. This locomotive was built at Brighton in 1946 and withdrawn in 1967. Multiple unit diesel set No.1015 waits to form the next express for Hastings. Platform 7/8 had been extended during the time when it could not be used, following the disastrous fire of April 1957 which destroyed the 1926 signal box. The temporary signal cabin was still intact in 1958, although by this time the new power box was open.

The 1959 view was taken from a train crossing over the river bridge into the station; what may appear to be marks near the church tower on the left are in fact gulls in flight. At platform 7 rebuilt light Pacific No.34037 'Clovelly' waits to leave on the 13.15, the last regular steam train to Ramsgate. At this time the roof had gone, but the former hotel remained; now it has been replaced by a modern office block, and Cannon Street presents a marked contrast in period styles.

21, 22, 23 St Johns, formerly South Eastern Railway (TQ 374764), on 16 July 1955, 10 May 1975 and 2 July 1976

This site was first traversed by the North Kent line of the SER in 1849. It became a junction in 1865 when the new main line was opened as far as Sevenoaks, and, in 1868, when this connected with the original main line at Tonbridge, St Johns became one of the busiest junctions on the SE. A station was opened in 1873 on the London side of the junction, taking its name from the adjacent church. It was a characteristic response to a challenge from the LCD, who opened the first part of their line to Greenwich Park in 1871, crossing over the SE at St Johns, with a nearby station called Lewisham Road. The LCD Greenwich Park line closed at the end of 1916, but in 1929 its western end was revived with a new spur leading down to the SE at Lewisham.

The 1955 view shows a scene which had changed little since 1929. The western of the two island platforms of the station is shown, with sidings occupying the space to the right. The abutment of the bridge which carried the LCD Greenwich Park branch is visible at the end of the siding, and beyond it, at an oblique angle, the connecting spur of 1929. By the 1960s the lines were unable to accommodate sufficient trains during peak hours to carry passengers in anything like reasonable comfort, and

various measures were put in hand to increase their carrying capacity. One of the projects was to provide what was in effect a flying junction at St Johns, using the existing bridge carrying the spur to the former Greenwich Park branch, and constructing a new spur on the site of the sidings to enable trains to join the main line to London Bridge.

By the time that the second photograph was taken in 1975 the western island platform of the station, the sidings and the abutment of the bridge which carried the Greenwich Park branch had all been obliterated. The site of the sidings was covered by an embankment sloping down towards the main line. Set 5309, a 4-EPB set, is forming an up Dartford loop train, running on the up local line. The new connection was brought into use on 15 April 1976, as shown in the third photograph. Grass was already established on the embankment, although its growth was not assisted by the dry heat of the summer of 1976. The up Orpington train on the local line was headed by 4-EPB Set No.5185. The eastern island platform serving the local lines, adorned with a traditional roof valance, remained unchanged, but the scene to the west had been transformed.

24, 25, 26 The junction at St Johns, formerly South Eastern Railway (TQ 376762), about 1910, 12 March 1955 and 2 July 1976.

As explained above, this was the junction of the North Kent and the South Eastern main line, with the LCD Greenwich Park branch carried over the top. The 1913 view is essentially South Eastern with a typical signal cabin in the fork of the junction. The signal on the down main line is cantilevered out from the post to aid sighting, and its red distant arm is fitted with a Coligny-Welch reflector to distinguish it from a stop signal. (These were removed when most Southern distant signals became yellow in the late 1920s.) The finials are not of standard SE pattern. The telegraph poles with their numerous crossbars are a striking feature. The photograph was taken from the end of the eastern platform, which served the local lines, and the end of the main line platform is visible on the right. Track details include a detonator placer on the down main line and a fouling bar to prevent improper movement of the trailing point on the up local line. But perhaps the most striking feature is the presence of three trains, a down local, an up North Kent and up express. The guard's brake on the down local is provided with a birdcage lookout, characteristic of the SE.

By 1955 a number of striking changes had occurred. In 1926 the tracks were electrified and in 1929 a new signal box, with colour light signals, was commissioned. (The signal wires were for the ground signals, one of which is visible beyond the end of the platform.) The bridge carrying the Greenwich Park branch had been removed, and in 1929 the new bridge carrying a spur down to join the North Kent and Mid Kent lines was brought into use for goods trains. The North Kent line was elevated so as to reduce the gradient on the spur. Passenger trains have used the spur since 1935, except during the Second World War. The photograph of 1955 shows, in the distance, a train running into the junction at Lewisham, with another train held on the spur until the first one has cleared the junction. Drivers received an indication of whether they were being sent onto the North Kent or the main line by the provision of a set of colour lights for each line, mounted on the same post.

Relief from overcrowding was sought in the early 1950s by lengthening the trains from 8 to 10 coaches, necessitating platform extensions to most of the former SE stations. St Johns was included, and the view of 1955 shows the recently completed extensions, with a notice indicating the stopping point for 10-coach trains at the end of each platform. The crossover shown in the 1913 view, was moved beyond the junction. A link between the two photographs is provided by the buffer stop at the end of the St Johns sidings and the double telegraph pole. By 1955 the eastern abutment of the Greenwich Park bridge had gone, but the end of the embankment, retained by a sleeper fence, was still to be seen.

The 1929 signal box was taken out of use in 1976, and was in fact disused but intact when the 1976 photograph was taken. This shows Set 5927 approaching on an up train from Hayes. The track layout remains unchanged. However, with only one platform surviving, the 10 coach stop sign has been moved to a lineside position, above the 30 mph speed restriction for trains running from the down local onto the main line. The other permanent speed restrictions are 40 mph from the down local to the North Kent, and 45 mph on the down through. The double colour lights have been replaced by a single 4-aspect signal with banner route indicator-signals No. L5 and L9 by signal L289. It will be noted that the signal on the down through No.L241 has been cantilevered out in much the same way as it was in 1913.

Reference to the 1955 view will show that its predecessor, signal No.L18, stood between the down and up through lines – that is, on the right hand side of the track. The two signals to the rear, L17 and L16, were also on the right, and in thick fog on the evening of 4 December 1957, the driver of a steam express to Ramsgate missed their indications of caution and only applied the brakes after his fireman shouted across to him that L18 was at danger. The express struck the rear of an electric train, standing with its brakes on, and the tender of the locomotive hit a column of the girder bridge which fell down into the train. 89 passengers and the guard of the electric train were killed. The collapsed bridge was restored by 13 January 1958, and the new span appears in the view of 1976. It is perhaps worth noting that Brigadier Langley, in his report on the accident, did not recommend the re-siting of L18, especially in view of the better visibility from the cabs of electric and diesel electric trains, which were already replacing steam on the Southern Region.

27, 28 Barbican Station, formerly Metropolitan Railway (TQ 321818), on 30 March 1954 and 18 June 1976

Barbican was opened on the Metropolitan's extension from Farringdon to Moorgate in 1865, and was originally named Aldersgate Street. It was a typical sub-surface Metropolitan station, built to take four tracks with side platforms and a central island platform; on either side were high, brick retaining walls with blind arcading. From the side walls sprang a magnificent roof with iron ribs, having a span of 80 ft and a length of 308 ft. The tracks on the north side were intended for Metropolitan and Great Western trains and were opened on 23 December 1865. Those on the south side were intended for other companies and, known as the Widened Lines, were opened early in March 1866. Originally the Metropolitan was built with mixed gauge track to take both the broad gauge trains of the Great Western, and the standard gauge of other companies. The GW agreed to run standard gauge trains from 1869, but the space for broad gauge tracks still remains on the Metropolitan.

At one time Barbican was served by the trains of six companies – the Metropolitan, the Metropolitan District, the Great Western, the Midland, the Great Northern, and the London, Chatham and Dover. The trains from the LCD ceased to run in 1916, and those of the GW at the outbreak of war in 1939. Partly as a result of bomb damage the services to the GN and Midland were withdrawn for most of the Second World War, but were restored with the return of peace. At the present time LT trains have replaced those of the Metropolitan and the District companies, the BR trains to the GN line were withdrawn in November 1976, but the services to the Midland are still maintained.

When the first view was taken the roof was still intact, and much of the original building survived over the end of the platform. The roof was demolished in 1955, its passing being celebrated by John Betjeman in his 'Monody on the Death of Aldersgate Street Station'. In the photograph a down train of Metropolitan compartment stock is just pulling into the island platform, and BR No.40037 is entering on a St Albans train, also consisting of compartment stock. This 2-6-2 locomotive was built at Derby in 1931 and withdrawn in 1961. A feature on the island platform is an LT type Next Train indicator. The 1976 view shows the station with its roof removed and buildings replaced. Canopies have been erected to shelter waiting passengers, but this is the only major change to the platforms. The brackets from which the ribs of the great iron roof sprung are still visible. Diesel replaced steam, with multiple-unit trains serving the Midland and

locomotive-hauled trains the Great Northern. The latter gave passengers their last opportunity to travel in suburban compartment stock on the King's Cross line. The photograph shows the 17.12 to Welwyn Garden City hauled by No.31203 (formerly No.D5627) built by Brush in 1960.

At present the only BR service to Aldersgate consists of the peak hour diesels to the Midland line, but when its electrification is completed a frequent service of BR electric trains is envisaged. This, however, will hardly provide the variety of the six companies of Victorian days.

29, 30, 31 Wood Lane Flyover, formerly Ealing and Shepherd's Bush Railway (TQ 226811), in September 1920, on 6 April 1957 and 2 July 1976

The Central London Railway, once known as the Twopenny Tube, was opened from the Bank to Shepherd's Bush in 1900. In order to accommodate exhibition traffic to the White City, passenger services were extended in 1908 to Wood Lane. The existing tube tunnel to the depot was used in one direction, and a new tunnel with an easier curve was constructed, crossing the original line, thus enabling trains to return to the City by running round a loop instead of reversing. The Ealing and Shepherd's Bush Railway was originally designed to give improved access from the Great Western Railway to the West London Railway near Shepherd's Bush. However it was agreed to add a spur at Wood Lane Junction, joining the Central London Railway, and enabling that company's trains to run through to Ealing Broadway.

A difficulty arose as the tube trains had run round the loop in an anti-clockwise direction at Wood Lane, and when leads were taken off from each side of the loop they ran on the right hand. To remedy this a flyover was provided at Wood Lane Junction, so that, before the shared tracks were reached, the tube trains were back on the left hand side. In 1938, in anticipation of more tube trains to serve the Ruislip Extension, the line from Wood Lane Junction to North Acton was quadrupled.

Subsequently GW and LT trains used different tracks, but the flyover was retained. By the early 1960s traffic from the GW to the West London line, including milk traffic, had declined sufficiently to enable the GW tracks on the Ealing and Shepherd's Bush lines to be removed, traffic reverting to the old route via North Pole Junction. But, in order to maintain normal running arrangements on the tube tracks west of Wood Lane, the flyover was still retained.

In 1920 a footbridge was provided crossing the Ealing and Shepherd's Bush Railway near the flyover, and all three photographs were taken from this viewpoint. The 1920 view shows the electrified lines with a 3-rail system, the live rail being in the centre. The down steam track from the West London line joins the down electric with an unworked trailing point. In slack periods the standard 6-car sets of the Central London Railway were divided at Wood Lane, and 3-car sets ran between there and Ealing Broadway. The photograph shows an eastbound train of 3 cars, of the type made up of motor cars of 1903 with the original trailer cars of 1900. An evocative feature is the grindstone alongside the platelayer's hut, used for sharpening the scythes for cutting lineside grass.

The 1957 view shows a westbound train for Ealing

approaching the flyover. The separate GW tracks of 1938 are in use, and coloured light signals have replaced semaphores. Standard London Transport 4-rail track has replaced 3-rail; this change was completed by 1940. At the same time many platforms were lengthened to take 8-car trains, and an 8-car train constructed for the London Electric Railway in 1927 appears in this view. The telegraph poles have hardly changed, but in 37 years the trees have grown and railwaymen's allotments have appeared. The 1976 view also shows a westbound train bound to Ealing, consisting of 8 cars built for London Transport in the 1960s. Nine years have brought little change to the electric lines, but houses are being constructed where the GW once ran.

32, 33 North Acton Junction, formerly Ealing and Shepherd's Bush Railway (TQ 203821), in September 1920 and 24 August 1957

Reference has already been made to the extension of Central line tube trains along new tracks, running parallel to the GW, as far as West Ruislip. Most of the work was completed before the war, but the track was temporarily removed, and it was 1947 before tube trains reached Greenford, with the final section to West Ruislip being opened in 1948.

The views of 1920 and 1957 are both taken looking down the line from the bridge carrying Park Royal Road. The 1920 view shows the E&SB diverging from the GW Birmingham direct line, with a connection enabling GW trains to gain their own tracks. The signal cabin, and the signals on the steam lines are of typical GW design. However, the signal which appears above the front of the tube train is one of the 3-position upper quadrants, which were installed on the E&SB. The 3-rail electric track has already been mentioned, and it will be noted that a central

live rail necessitated elaborate arrangements in the track crossing in the foreground. To the right the wooden cooling towers of the GW electric power station which supplied the E&SB are visible above the roof line.

By 1957 the Birmingham line had been slewed to the north, to give room for a burrowing junction between the tube train lines to Ealing and to Ruislip. A new GW signal box in their 1930s style had been provided. In addition to the steel bridge carrying the Ealing line over the west-bound Ruislip there was a concrete bridge visible to the left of the signal box, carrying a private siding. In 1957 everything on the GW side was still traditional, with manually operated points, semaphore signals and a steam-hauled train. One interesting survival on the electric side is the oil lamp on the back of the tube train to West Ruislip. The view illustrates plainly the contrast between two types of London railway.

2 South West from London

34, 35, 36 New Malden Station, formerly London & South Western Railway (TQ 214687), about 1910, in 1936 and on 30 March 1974

The first section of the London and Southampton Railway was opened in 1838 between Nine Elms and Woking. A station named Coombe & Malden was provided about 1¼ miles north of the village of Malden in 1846; it was about the same distance south of Coombe. A third settlement, called New Malden, grew up around the station. This situation led to a succession of station re-namings as follows: in 1859 to New Malden and Coombe, in 1862 to Coombe and Malden, in 1912 to Malden (for Coombe), and finally, in 1957, to New Malden. In 1869 two extra tracks were projected beyond the site of Raynes Park. After passing through New Malden on the south side, they descended to pass below the main line, which was carried on an embankment west of the station, and made an end-on junction with an earlier line at Kingston. This necessitated changes in the station to approximately its present form, with two side platforms and a central island. By 1884 quadrupling of the main line had extended to Hampton Court Junction, with the centre tracks used for through traffic and the outside tracks for local traffic. To avoid up trains from Kingston having to cross the two down lines on the level, a new spur was constructed on the north side of the main line embankment, thus producing a burrowing junction. The position of the passenger station, on the main line at the point of transition from embankment to cutting, provided no convenient site for a goods yards, and this was opened on the Kingston line near Malden Crossing Signal Box. It was closed in 1964.

The first view shows an up commuter's train arriving on the through line. It consists of a close-coupled set of LSW coaches hauled by a 4-4-2 tank locomotive of Adams design. Suits with flowers in the button hole, fresh culled from suburban gardens, are almost universal, but the obligatory headgear is fairly evenly divided between bowlers and boaters. The eye catching anomalies among the passengers are a man wearing a cloth cap, and no less than three women. At the country end of the station a typical LSW bracket signal with lattice post is visible. Reading from left to right the arms apply to the following:

Down Local to Kingston, Down Local, Down Local to Down Through, Down Through to Kingston, Down Through to Down Local, Down Through. The two arms controlling routes that did not involve diversions were placed at a higher level than the other four. The top of the signal box is visible over the canopy on the island platform, and the typical LSW stop signal appears on the right. Other period features are the overhead telegraph lines and the gas lamps.

The 1936 view was taken from the country end of the down local platform after the conversion to 4-aspect colour light signals. The signal for the down local is at the platform end, and that for the down through is canti-levered out over the track to which it applies. Diversions, in the first case to the Kingston line or the down through (one to the left, one to the right) and in the second to the Kingston line or the down local (both to the left), are indicated by white lights appearing above the coloured lights of the signals. As was common practice on the Southern, the existing signal box and some manual operations were retained. The arms have been removed from the bracket signal, which was described above. Other visible changes include the electrification of the lamps and the track, electric train services on the third rail system having been introduced in 1916. The numbers on the lamp post indicate the stopping place for electric trains of 6 or 8 coaches.

New Malden suffered bomb damage during the war and the third view, taken from a train on the down local line, shows new canopies on both side platforms. The central island serving the through lines is now rarely used and has no cover. Detailed changes include the substitution of Southern Railway concrete lamp posts for metal ones, with characteristic white lampshades. Chaired track has been replaced by continuous welded rail on concrete sleepers. The signal cabin and the coloured light signals are unchanged. A significant development is the large office block on the left, located in what was mainly a residential district.

37, 38, 39 West of Woking, formerly London & South Western Railway (SU 998582), about 1920, on 27 August 1966 and 24 August 1976

The section of the Southampton line between Woking and Winchfield was opened in 1838. Beyond Woking the line climbed at 1 in 326 into a long cutting. Widening to four tracks was completed by 1904. However, the views taken at this point were chosen mainly to show the development of trains. The 1920 and 1976 views were both taken looking to London from the footbridge which spans the main line west of Woking Station. Woking Junction Signal Box is visible between the Down Through and Local lines in the first view. This was replaced, together with the East and Yard Boxes, by a new box with coloured light signals in 1936. The coaches in the yard are mostly examples of LSW compartment bogie coaches, while the wagons include one from the Great Central Railway. According to the head code the train is a down Plymouth express, double-headed by locomotives Nos.416 and 685. The train engine, No.685 of Adams T6 class, was built at Nine Elms in 1896 and withdrawn in 1936. The pilot, No.416 of Drummond's L12 class, was also constructed at Nine Elms, with a working life from 1904 to 1953. The 1976 view shows a down Bournemouth express in roughly the

same position. It is made up of three 4-coach units. The usual formation for the Bournemouth and Weymouth line was one powered and two unpowered sets, but in this case all 3 sets were powered. The leading unit, Set No.7438 of the Southern Region 4-ClG class (BR Class 421/2) was built by BREL at York in 1972. Beyond the train, the flood lights of what has become a Permanent Way Depot are a feature on the skyline.

The 1966 view was taken from a point west of the footbridge from the front of a diesel multiple-unit train. The signals are those installed in 1936, of the same design as that illustrated in photograph No. 35. The track is flat bottomed with wooden sleepers and a live rail. An up boat train from Southampton is passing on the up through line. Special sets were used for this traffic, and it will be seen that the first two vehicles are baggage vans. The locomotive is No.73080 'Merlin' of the BR Class Five Standard design, built at Derby Works in 1955 and withdrawn in 1966. Boat trains have declined in recent years, but were a familiar feature of the Southampton line in the 1950s and 1960s.

40, 41 East Croydon Station, formerly London, Brighton and South Coast Railway (TQ 329658), on 9 November 1954 and 24 July 1975

East Croydon was opened on the main line from London to Brighton in 1841. It was on the section used by both the South Eastern and the Brighton company's trains, but was an LBSC station. An annexe from which the SE were excluded, named New Croydon, was opened in 1862. In addition to local LBSC trains, it was served by Great Eastern trains from the East London line and London & North Western trains from the West London line. From the 1890s, although the division between the LBSC platform and the jointly served platforms was retained, East Croydon had assumed almost its present form. Basically, this consists of three island platforms numbered from west to east and serving the following tracks: 1 (Up Local), 2 (Down Local), 3 (Up Loop), 4 (Up Through), 5 (Down Through), 6 (Down Loop).

Both of the photographs were taken from platform 2 looking towards London. This island platform was treated as a separate LBSC station, named New Croydon from 1862 until 1909, then East Croydon Local until 1924, in which year, with the advent of the Southern Railway, the main and local stations were united. The first view records the period between March 1954 and May 1955 when Gloucester Road SB was open with colour light signals but when the two East Croydon boxes were still using semaphores. Thus the gantry for the Up Loop has lower quadrant arms, that on the left for movement to the Up Local and that on the right for the Up Through, together with ringed arms for freight lines, and the colour light distant signals for Gloucester Road. A curved, concrete bracket is in position, preparatory to replacing the signal

gantry. Both new and old signal boxes are shown, although the new box was not yet in use. A manually operated ground signal is visible on the right foreground, while its electrically operated replacement is in the process of being installed. Electric train services on the overhead wire system commenced in 1925, and one of the gantries used for supporting the wires may be seen beyond the old signal box; this was retained as a signal gantry. The overhead wires were replaced by the live rail in 1928, but the sidings between the local and main stations were not electrified. Gas lighting continued into the days of electric traction, even if the lamps were suspended from standard Southern concrete posts. Steam traction is attested to by the water crane at the end of the platform, and the large water tank. Other details shown are overhead telegraph wires and the loudspeakers of a public address system.

The view of 1975 is taken a little further from the end of the platform. The curved concrete signal bracket, together with the new signal box and its associated equipment, was brought into use in May 1955. Features which have survived include the platforms and their canopies, and the gantry for the wires of the overhead electrification. New features include electric lighting and the bridge connecting the platforms (although passengers continue to use the subway). The water tank and water column have been removed, but the most striking change is the removal of the sidings. These marked very clearly the division between New Croydon, the station used exclusively by the LBSC, and East Croydon shared by the LBSC and the SER. Now the old division is represented by an empty space.

40

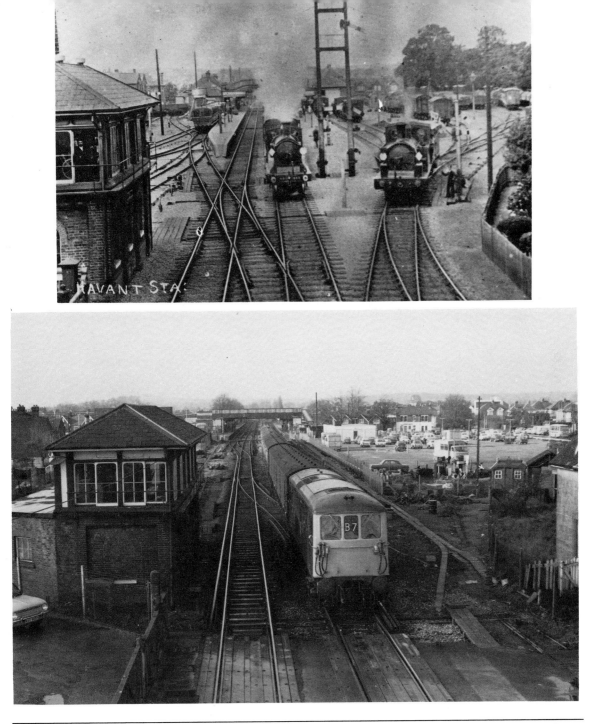

42, 43 East of Havant Station, formerly London Brighton and South Coast Railway (SU 721066), about 1908 and on 3 February 1977

Havant Station was opened in 1847 on the line between Chichester and Portsmouth. At this time the Brighton company's route to Portsmouth lay via Brighton and Chichester, and this competed with the LSW route via Gosport. In 1848 the LSW opened their line from Fareham, on the Gosport line, to Cosham, from which point they shared the LBSC line into Portsmouth. The Portsmouth Direct Railway was an independent concern linking the LSW Godalming branch to the LBSC Portsmouth line at Havant. The LSW, as lessees of the Portsmouth Direct, felt that they were entitled to the running powers between Havant and Cosham granted to the leasors; the LBSC took a different view, thus precipitating the notorious 'Battle of Havant' in 1859. This ended in an agreement for the pooling of receipts from Portsmouth traffic, and subsequently LSW trains ran over the LBSC between Cosham and Havant without being the cause of any further disagreement.

Havant Station was opened on a flat site between two level crossings, north of the small market town with its long established leather and parchment industries. By 1889 traffic had developed sufficiently to justify rebuilding on the same site. The electrification of the former LSW Direct Portsmouth route in 1937 and the LBSC route in 1938 encouraged further growth, and a second, more radical, rebuilding of the station took place. The level crossing at the Portsmouth end of the station was closed and replaced by a separate footbridge and a road bridge over the railway. The new station buildings, in typical Southern 'Odeon' style, were constructed to the west of the old station. However, the bay platform for the Hayling Island branch of 1867 was retained, together with the goods yard. Two signal boxes were closed but the Junction box which adjoined the eastern of the two level crossings was maintained and extended. The new platforms were set back to allow for two platform and two through roads. As re-equipped, the Junction box operated the points at the Portsmouth end of the platform loops electrically, although the points and crossing gates adjoining the box continued to be worked mechanically. Semaphore signals on the main line were replaced by colour lights. Since 1938 the main changes have been the closure of the Hayling Island branch, in 1963, and of the goods yard, in 1969. On the credit side the London expresses which used to pass on the through lines now call at Havant.

Both the photographs were taken from the footbridge adjoining the level crossing at the east end of the station, looking to the west. The first view shows the old station

and, although the western level crossing is obscured, its position is indicated by the houses beyond the goods yard. The Hayling Island branch train is in its bay. The junction signal box appears to be a typical Saxby and Farmer design, and the signalman and the wheel for operating the crossing gates are visible. The signal with its two posts, at the end of the down platform, is unusually interesting. The left-hand post carried four arms, reading from top to bottom: up LBSC West Coast line, Down home, up LBSC West Coast line (co-acting with arm above), shunt ahead signal (the top arm is off the photograph). The right-hand post carried the Up Portsmouth Direct, the distant signal for Havant North SB, the Up Portsmouth Direct (co-acting with the arm above) and a shunt signal. The photograph shows the arms pulled off for the Portsmouth Direct line. Other signal posts are visible for the Hayling Island branch and in the goods yard. The fence protecting the garden of Crossing Keeper's House No.66 appears on the right hand side. An LSW tank locomotive is shunting in the yard, on a pick-up freight train. The Up LSW express is hauled by a Drummond 4-4-0 locomotive of the K10 class.

By 1977 the tracks had been removed from the goods yard and the Hayling Island bay. The goods shed and the Hayling Island platform were demolished in 1972. The signal box is shown as rebuilt in 1938; the lower windows were bricked up during the war as an air raid precaution. Somewhat surprisingly the crossing keeper's house survives, although the neat wooden palings have been replaced by concrete posts and chain link fencing. An up Parcels train has passed the station on the up through line. The locomotive No.73135 (formerly No.E6042) of the electro-diesel Class 73 was constructed by English Electric and Vulcan Foundry in 1966. The extinction of a branch line and a goods yard, accompanied by a development of passenger traffic, is not uncharacteristic of the Southern Region.

44, 45, 46 Royal Victoria Station, Clarence Yard, Gosport (SU 618004), about 1900, on 10 July 1965 and 11 September 1976

This was a private station provided in a Royal Dockyard for the use of Queen Victoria. The Queen and the Prince Consort purchased Osborne House on the Isle of Wight and started a major rebuilding programme in 1845. Prince Albert realised that a simple extension of the LSW Gosport line across a road and through the fortifications of the Clarence Yard would greatly facilitate royal journeys to the Island. Only a few years earlier there had been adamant refusal to allow the railway to penetrate the fortifications, and the extension was a striking testimony to the potency of royal influence. It must be stressed however that its use was confined to Admiralty traffic and royal journeys. It was opened in September 1845 and was last used for a Royal train in 1901. The very special arrangements were described by G.P. Neele in the *Railway*

Magazine for December 1906. (Mr Neele was Superintendent of the line for the LNWR, but usually made the journey of 625 miles from Gosport to Ballater in Scotland.) With the death of the Queen, Royal visits to Osborne ended, and the sole traffic of the Royal Victoria Station ended with them. The line to the Dockyard continued in use for Admiralty traffic, but the station was converted to a store.

The first view shows the station, as used by the Queen. There was a single track with no run-round facilities. The side platform was 520 feet long, but frequently the Royal train exceeded this length. Normally steps were provided for the coaches beyond the end of the platform. However for the funeral train a temporary extension of 50 feet was constructed. A curtain wall ran along the back of the platform, with generous lighting provided by round-headed windows with iron glazing bars incorporating coronets. Protection from weather was achieved by an overall roof supported by iron columns on the side opposite to the curtain wall. Although the royal salons were marshalled near the centre of the train, the waiting rooms were at the north end of the station, near to the pier to which the royal yacht was secured.

The second view shows the station with the track removed and converted to a store. This was carried out by filling in the space occupied by the track, using the iron columns to support a corrugated iron wall and boarding up the ends. The waiting rooms, which projected beyond the curtain wall, were demolished. In 1971, with the exception of a short length of the curtain wall, the Royal Victoria Station was demolished. This section of wall appears in the photograph of 1976, with three of the original windows with their iron glazing bars and coronets. One window and the openings which led from the platforms to the waiting rooms were bricked up when the station was in use as a store. It is fortunate that at least something has survived of what must have been the most private and least used station in Britain.

47, 48, 49 Yarmouth Station, formerly Freshwater, Yarmouth and Newport Railway (SZ 357894), in September 1920, 28 August 1953 and 21 June 1977

The Freshwater, Yarmouth and Newport Railway was one of the smallest complete railways in Britain, with a total of 12 route miles and with two locomotives. Its title described its route, which included a junction with the Isle of Wight Central Railway at Newport. Freight working with a contractor's locomotive began in 1888, and in the following year an agreement was reached with the Isle of Wight Central, who provided a passenger service. This continued until 1913, when the FYN, aggrieved at the rate charged by the IWC, decided to provide their own service with two locomotives and twelve coaches. For a short time the FYN operated in complete rather than splendid isolation, its trains being debarred from the IWC Newport Station. In 1923 the newly-formed Southern took over all the island railways, and the FYN was integrated with the rest of the system. Before the First World War some progress was made with plans for a tunnel linking the LSW Lymington branch to the FYN, and it has been suggested that this was one reason for the 'Fresh' asserting its independence in 1913. Had this scheme materialised it might have saved the Freshwater line, but in the event it closed in 1953

The first view shows Yarmouth in FYN days. Although it was provided with a loop, all trains normally used the platform on the up side. The staff section was from Ningwood to Freshwater, with Yarmouth as an intermediate block post. The signal box (visible to the left of the haystack) controlled the semaphore signals on the running lines, and also the freight sidings, which ran at the back of the box. The track is laid with the original flat-bottom rail (64 lb per yard) on wooden sleepers with shingle ballast. The hay crop would be harvested from the sides of the line and, as the 'Fresh' did not operate any horses, the haystack was presumably sold. The modest brick building on the up platform included a booking office and waiting room. Amenities for those using the platform included seats, a lamp and, if required, buckets of water or sand for fire fighting.

The second view shows the impact of the Southern. The loop line, signal box and signals have all been removed. The track has been relaid with standard bullhead rail laid in chairs. Although not visible, the siding is still in position, and was often the stabling point for cattle trucks, as cattle were sometimes sent from Yarmouth to the mainland. A substantial platform trolley has appeared but the fire buckets seem to have vanished. The train approaching is typical of the period, with an LSWR O2 class 0-4-4T locomotive, with 4 coaches, 2 former LBSC and 2 SECR, thus representing all 3 constituents of the Southern Railway.

The third view shows Yarmouth Station in 1977, twenty-four years after its closure. The platform and building survive, the site being used by a local youth club. The shingle ballast that once supported the track now provides a good footpath. An adjoining thoroughfare is still called Station Road and, although nobody under 24 has ever seen a train in Yarmouth, the railway is well remembered.

50, 51 Sandown Station, formerly Isle of Wight Railway (SZ 593844), on 20 August 1922 and 27 May 1967

The Isle of Wight Railway was the only company with a line on a lucrative route. It linked Ryde, Sandown, Shanklin and Ventnor. When it first opened in 1864 it terminated at Shanklin at one end and on the outskirts of Ryde at the other (although from 1871 a tramway closed the gap between the Railway station and the Pier). Extension to Ventnor, including a 1312 yard tunnel, was achieved in 1866, and the gap at the Ryde end was closed by the LSW and LBSC companies in 1880. Sandown became a junction when a line was opened from the edge of Newport in 1875 (it was 1879 before it was connected to the Isle of Wight Central Station at Newport). The up platform was converted to an island, with Newport trains using the outer face up until the closure of the Newport line in 1956. The line from Ryde to Shanklin was electrified in 1967 on the 630V d.c. system.

The first view was taken in the last year of independence

of the Isle of Wight Railway. Sandown had been in use as a passing place since the opening of the station in 1864 and the signal cabin is visible, projecting above the canopy on the up platform. The down train is headed by 'Bonchurch', a 2-4-0 tank locomotive of the Isle of Wight Railway's basically standard design, delivered new from Beyer, Peacock in 1883. The IWR did not number their locomotives, but the Southern gave 'Bonchurch' the number W18 before it was scrapped in 1928. While the IWR purchased new locomotives, they relied on second-hand coaches, and those in the photograph were from a London underground line – the Metropolitan. They were non-bogie eight-wheelers which became available when the Metropolitan was electrified in 1905. The station buildings are visible over the roofs of the coaches, with the company's offices adjoining.

The second view was taken in 1967, shortly after the

46

introduction of electric services. The station buildings show little change, but the live rail has been added to the chaired tracks. The trains maintain the Island tradition of second-hand rolling stock, but in this case it is from the London Transport tube system as compared to the Metropolitan. Second-hand London Transport stock was found to be acceptable for the Island loading gauge, with its electrical control gear in a suitable position for maintenance at the Ryde Works. Cars were purchased in 1965, and in 1967 6 three-car sets (classified by the Southern as 3-TIS and by BR as Class 486) and 6 four-car sets (classified as 4-VEC and 485) were placed in service. (The Southern classification reflects the Roman name of the Isle of Wight, Vectis.) The photograph shows the end of 3-TIS Set O36 on an up train, and 3-TIS Set O32 on a down. In each case motored cars are shown; on Set O36 Isle of Wight Car No.11 (formerly London Transport No.3705), and on Set O32 Car No.3 (formerly London Transport No.3251). Both came from the batch supplied by Metropolitan Cammell between 1932 and 1935. Minor details include the red disc indicating rear of train on O36, and, as the sets are directional, the D appearing near the end of the shallow clerestory, marking the Shanklin end of the train. Some alterations, such as the demolition of the Isle of Wight company's offices and part of the station canopy are not shown on the 1967 photograph. However, it does show a view which could only be seen on the Isle of Wight, even down to such details as the continued use of shingle for track ballast.

52, 53, 54 Winchester Chesil Station, formerly Great Western Railway (SU 488292), on 8 May 1954, 10 July 1965 and 27 October 1972

Most of Hampshire was occupied by the LSWR, but both the GWR and the LBSCR operated penetrating lines. One of the Great Western penetrations was achieved by virtue of working the Didcot, Newbury and Southampton Railway. This independent company opened its line from Didcot to the GW at Newbury in 1882, and from Newbury to a temporary terminal in Winchester in 1885. The original plan was to construct an independent line through to Southampton, but instead an arrangement was reached whereby a spur was built from the LSWR main line at Shawford to an end junction with the DNSR at Winchester. The Great Western operated the DNSR, and from 1891 GW trains, hauled from Winchester by LSW locomotives, ran through to Southampton. Between the wars, under conditions of reduced competition, the GW locomotives remained on the trains. The DNS was closed to passengers between Winchester and Newbury in 1960 and for all through traffic in 1964. The last section

to survive, from Shawford Junction to Winchester Chesil Goods Depot, was closed in 1966.

As explained above, when the DNS reached Winchester in 1885 its future was uncertain, and it confined itself to erecting a temporary station at Winchester. It did, however, provide a station master's house with the characteristic DNS gabled windows ornamented with barge boards, which appears in the background of all three photographs. Passengers had to be content with temporary accommodation until 1892, when permanent buildings bearing all the marks of the operating, as opposed to the owning, company were opened. The low turrets, like truncated pyramids, adorned with orna- mental ironwork were repeated at other points on the GW system. Other distinctive GW features were the use of red, yellow and blue bricks and blue paving tiles for the platforms. The 1954 view shows the station substantially

as it appeared throughout its normal working life from 1892 to 1960.

The DNS had a single track for most of the way between Winchester and Newbury, and up and down trains are shown passing, with the up train running into the tunnel. On the typical GW coaches of the down train to Southampton such features as the brackets for supporting roof boards are visible. This train obscures the down platform, which was a simple affair, reached by a footbridge and provided with a waiting room. The canopy on the up platform was unusually elaborate, with a clerestory with top lights running almost the whole length of the buildings. A reminder of the war time blackout is provided by the broad white bands on the gas lamp post, and on the pillars supporting the canopy. The Big Four railways are represented by a poster board headed 'LNER'.

The 1965 view was taken after closure to through freight traffic but at a time when there was still rail access to the Winnall Sidings about $\frac{1}{2}$ mile north of the station. Changes include the removal of the footbridge and canopy, and many of the coping bricks on the up platform. The signalling is retained, with typical GW lower quadrant arms for both platforms. (A power system was installed experimentally in 1923 but normal manual working was re-established later.) The white painted patches on the bricks of the tunnel assisted in the sighting of the two signals.

The final view of 1972 was taken after the withdrawal of all services, the sale of the building to Winchester City Council, and the onset of demolition. The platforms are overgrown and the tunnel mouth is closed with gates. The slates were sold and the bricks went for hard core, but the ornamental ironwork and finely moulded window sills and lintels were retained for exhibition in the City Museum. In this way citizens of the future may be reminded that Winchester once had a second station.

55, 56, 57 Shawford Junction, formerly LSWR (SU 473262), about 1925, on 10 July 1965 and 23 September 1976

As explained previously, the LSWR parried the DNSR thrust towards Southampton by agreeing to a spur from their main line at Shawford to Winchester, opened in 1891. The spur was only 2 miles long but it included an impressive viaduct of 23 arches across the valley of the River Itchen. Passenger traffic on the DNSR ended in 1960, through traffic in 1964, and the last section from Shawford to Winchester was closed in 1966.

The first view shows the junction much as it would have appeared when opened. St Catherine's Hill on the east side of the Itchen Valley is visible and below it the impressive Hockley Viaduct, the longest in Hampshire. The junction is conventional with a flat crossing, locking arrangements on the facing points and protected by lower quadrant signals. Much of the fencing has wooden posts, but concrete posts, later to achieve something approaching universality in rural areas on the Southern, are visible in the right foreground. Shawford Junction SB was a typical LSWR box with a hipped roof and windows with small panes in close set glazing bars.

The second view shows the important change which took place during the war. During 1942 and 1943, in preparation for the invasion of Europe, the capacity of the DNS was increased partly by doubling the track, and elsewhere by the lengthening of passing places. At Shawford a new down track was laid, enabling trains from the DNS to reach the down relief line beyond Shawford Station without having to wait for a path on the down main at the junction. There was a consequential alter-ation to the home signal, to which a bracket with a semaphore arm was attached, to cover the new track. This appears on the 1965 view, together with some later changes. These include the 30 mph permanent speed restriction and the new concrete hut for permanent way staff. Flat bottomed track appears on the main line, but the war-time new line retains its chairs. The down express of Bulleid coaches is hauled by rebuilt Merchant Navy class No.35017 'Belgian Marine', built at Eastleigh in 1945 and withdrawn in 1966.

The third view shows the post electrification scene. Shawford ceased to be a junction in 1966 and the signal box and signals have been removed. Of the two tracks of the main line one has been relaid with concrete sleepers and continuous welded rail, and both carry a live rail. The wartime link line continues in use, but instead of being reached from the DNS there is now a turnout just south of the bridge from which the photograph was taken, to which the 50 mph permanent speed restriction applies. It will be noted that the overhead telegraph line has gone underground. The train is the 10.46 Waterloo to Bournemouth, motive power being provided by a 4-REP Set forming the rear 4 coaches of the train. It is propelling two 4-TC sets, with Set 409 forming the leading unit. These sets were constructed from existing stock for the electrification of 1967. With the closure of a secondary line, the demise of traditional signalling and electrification of a main line, the scenes at Shawford summarise some of the main changes on British railways.

58, 59, 60 Eastleigh Station, formerly LSWR (SU 457191), on 31 October 1972 and two views on 18 June 1976

When the section of the London and Southampton Railway between Southampton and Winchester was opened in 1839, Eastleigh was the only intermediate station. It rapidly became one of the most important junctions on the line, with the Gosport branch of 1842 serving Portsmouth from 1848, and the Salisbury branch opening in 1847. The LSWR purchased a large quantity of land on the east side of the line, to which the carriage and wagon works were removed from Nine Elms in 1889 and the locomotive works in 1909. In 1903 the engine shed for the Southampton area which had been at Northam was transferred to Eastleigh which, before the First World War, relied almost entirely on the railway for its existence. Its development is reflected in the successive names of the station, which bore the name of the nearby village of Bishopstoke until 1852, became Bishopstoke Junction until 1889, and Eastleigh and Bishopstoke until 1923. The present buildings belong to three main periods. The original building, although obscured by later develop-ments, survives on the up side. Considerable enlargement took place about 1895, when the up platform became an island. Finally, at the time of electrification, new buildings were completed on the down side in 1967.

The three photographs were all taken on the up platform. The first was taken at the Southampton end, and shows a survival of the pre-nationalisation era. The engine shed and locomotive yard were situated beyond the overbridge, on the east side of the line (the left-hand side beyond the bridge in the picture). The official route for enginemen and others arriving by train from the station to the yard was by the public road and over the bridge. However, the quickest route was along the tracks, but the heavy traffic made this dangerous and is the reason for the slightly authoritarian notice. It survived from the early days of the Southern Railway until 1973, well into the days of electrification and British Rail.

The next view shows the three periods represented by Eastleigh Station. The new building of 1967 on the down platform is visible beyond the locomotive. The 1895 period is represented by the covered footbridge, with its dwarf dormers with louvres so characteristic of LSW architectural style at that time. Finally, the part of the canopy shown was erected shortly after the opening of the station. The train is a down Freightliner with containers for Southampton Docks, hauled by Class 47 No.47536 constructed at Crewe Works in 1965. All four tracks consist of continuous welded rail, with wooden guards screening the live rails on the platform roads. Power signalling has been in use at Eastleigh since November 1966, but a banner repeater for a colour light signal is visible on the footbridge.

As mentioned, one of the buildings and the adjoining platform canopy formed part of the original station. There is good archaeological evidence for the age of the canopy, as the pillars are marked with the name of the iron founder and the date as follows: J. LANKESTER SOUTHAMPTON 1841. Unfortunately, successive layers of paint over the last 135 years have obscured the marking, but the accompanying photograph at least indicates its position. The iron founder who thought that there might be interest in the date of his work 135 years after its completion was not wrong.

61, 62 Signal gantry at Northam, Southampton, formerly LSWR (SU 428125), in 1902 and on 9 February 1977

When the line to Bournemouth was electrified the intention was to eliminate semaphore signalling. This has almost been carried out, but lack of available capital has led to a prolonged life of several miles of traditional signalling in Southampton. Among the boxes surviving is that controlling the junction at Northam, which is provided with an impressive gantry for the down lines. This was erected in 1902 when the line between St Denys and Northam Junction was quadrupled. The first view shows it being lifted into position. Two hand cranes are lifting the main girder onto the upright columns. Assisting the operation is 0-6-0 saddle tank No. 330 of the LSW 330 class which was constructed by Beyer, Peacock, in 1876 and scrapped in 1924.

A visit to the site on a wet morning in February 1977 showed the gantry still in use, the most conspicuous change being the provision of upper quadrant semaphore arms. The five arms to the right apply to the running roads as follows: Down Relief to Sidings, Down Relief to Main Line, Down Relief to Branch, Down Through to Main Line, Down Through to Branch. Four of the posts also carry distant signals, those for the main line being operated from Chapel SB and those for the Branch from Southampton SB. The latter are operated by electric motors. The three

left hand posts apply to tracks in Mulfords Siding, with theatre-type indicators to show whether the road is set for the main line or the branch. In fact this nomenclature is now out of date, for since 1970 the branch which diverges on a curve so sharp as to necessitate a 15 mph speed restriction has been called the main line, and the former main line became the branch. This re-designation was based on the fact that the branch, leading to Bournemouth through Southampton Station, was the *de facto* main line. However, there was no re-adjustment of the relative heights of the signals, as on the Northam gantry the arms for the former branch line were already at a higher level than those for the original main line.

The background to the gantry also shows detailed changes. Some of the terraced housing has been wall painted, with tiles replacing roofing slates. The sleeper boundary has been replaced by chain-link fencing. Ground signals are in evidence and, although not distinguishable on the photograph, live rails have been added to the running lines. A more unusual sight are the two portable 'sentry boxes' of the type once used by fogmen, but now in general use by permanent way staff. The whole scene has a vintage railway atmosphere.

63, 64 Canute Road Level Crossing, Southampton, formerly LSWR (SU 426110), on 5 April 1959 and 3 February 1973

The terminal at Southampton was opened in 1840, and two years later the tracks were extended across Canute Road to the newly-opened Outer Dock. A second level crossing was necessary to serve the Inner Dock opened in 1856. A third crossing was used to reach the Town Quay and Royal Pier. When first opened in 1847 this led to a turntable on the far side of the road, but in 1871 a new line curving across the road ended the inconvenience of turntables. Gates were provided on both sides of the road, to protect railway and dock property respectively, but these were not conventional level crossing gates and did not draw across the road. When necessary, road traffic was stopped by flagmen, while trains crossed at a very cautious speed. In addition to freight traffic, all three crossings have carried boat trains, and the 1856 crossing carried a number of flying-boat trains. (The flying-boat terminal at Berth 50 was in use from 1948 until 1958.) This is the only crossing of the three which survives.

The first view shows an up Channel Islands Boat Express on the original crossing of 1842. This was a single line crossing leaving the docks by what is now No.3 Gate, between the National Westminster Bank and the new Dock House. The flagman is visible to the left of the cylinder of the locomotive, his presence reinforced with a notice that 'Trains Cross Here'. There were no signals on the docks railway system, but running lines commenced

on the railway side of the road, and the signal for the boat train is visible on the right. The bracket signal for the two tracks of the 1856 crossing is visible in front of the former South Western Hotel. On this occasion the locomotive crossing the road was Lord Nelson class No.30855 'Robert Blake', built at Eastleigh in 1928 and withdrawn in 1961. The BR passenger steamer service ended in 1964, and in 1966 the 1842 level crossing was removed.

The first view shows the 1842 crossing from the east; the second shows the 1856 crossing from the west. This still carries a modest freight traffic and the occasional boat train for the Ocean Terminal. The train shown was in fact going to the Ocean Terminal but, as the inconspicuous name plate on the left hand lamp bracket shows, was a special hired by the LCGB for a rail tour. The method of operating the crossings has not changed over the years, and the flagman is visible. The train was propelled by Class 33/1 No.6511 (now 33101) built by the BRCW in 1960. It consisted of 2 4-TC sets with a Buffet Car in between. One end of Set 404 appears in the photograph. The telegraph pole, which appears in both views, probably remains because it has not been considered worthwile to move it. At one time, especially when the horse trams used Canute Road to reach the Floating Bridge, railway and road traffic was very much in each other's way, but the amount of rail traffic using the crossings is now moderate.

65, 66 Steamer Terminal, Southampton Docks (SU 427109), on 5 April 1959 and 3 February 1973

Passenger stations are normally designed for transfer between road and rail, but exceptionally the transfer is from rail to water. If international traffic is involved, in addition to the platform for the train and the berth for the steamer, accommodation has to be provided for Customs and Immigration Control. The largest station of this type in Southampton Docks was opened in 1950, and named the Ocean Terminal. The facilities provided for the cross-channel steamers were comparatively modest, both in terms of size and luxury. Compared with transatlantic liners, cross-channel steamers carried fewer passengers, who spent less time aboard. After the withdrawal of the railway steamers the buildings of the cross-channel terminal were adapted to new uses, mostly connected with the operations of the roll-on roll-off fleet of Thoresens, who replaced BR on the Le Havre route.

The first view shows the terminal in use with a boat train about to depart. By this time all the locomotives of the Lord Nelson class were based on Eastleigh, and boat trains were one of their regular assignments. The train shown here, with No.30855, was photographed again as it crossed Canute Road (see photograph No.63). Tracks of

the docks railway system are prominent in the photograph, including a length of track set in a road surface, and a crossing. A booking office was provided for steamer passengers arriving by road, and as indicated by the cars, by 1959 their number was increasing. The entrance to the terminal was marked 'Channel Islands, Havre and St Malo Services'. The service to the Channel Islands was concentrated on Weymouth in 1961, and the French services ended in 1964; fortunately for the port of Southampton, Thoresens introduced their roll-on roll-off services to Le Havre and Cherbourg in the same year.

The second view shows the terminal in use by roll-on roll-off services. When the Channel Islands service was transferred to Weymouth, the sign over the entrance was altered to 'Continental Booking Office'. This was formed by letters affixed to the stone, and when they were removed a ghost-like impression remained. The railway tracks were lifted, and re-arrangement took place inside the building. However, as the two views show, the railway steamer terminal has been adapted without any great change to its external appearance.

67, 68, 69 Southampton Station, formerly LSWR (SU 414122), about 1920, on 17 September 1966 and 22 January 1977

The Southampton and Dorchester Railway was opened in 1847. The company had agreed to the inclusion in their authorising Act of a clause requiring them to build and adequately serve a station at Blechynden Terrace, Southampton, to accommodate the residents of the superior housing going up to the north and west of the town. There were problems, but in 1850 the temporary wooden station was replaced by a two-platform establishment named Blechynden. In 1858 a new spur at Northam enabled trains to avoid calling at the terminus, and to cope with this the platforms at Blechynden were extended and it was re-named Southampton West End. In order to improve schedules it was undesirable for any trains to be directed in and out of the original Southampton station after the direct route to Bournemouth had been opened in 1888.

In 1895 a new station, named Southampton West, was opened immediately to the west of Southampton West End and on the opposite side of the level crossing. This was substantially rebuilt and its name changed to Southampton Central in 1935. Finally, a year after the closure of the terminus in 1966, what had begun as a suburban wayside station became Southampton.

All three views are taken from the public footbridge which originally adjoined the level crossing at the east end of the station. The first view shows Southampton West

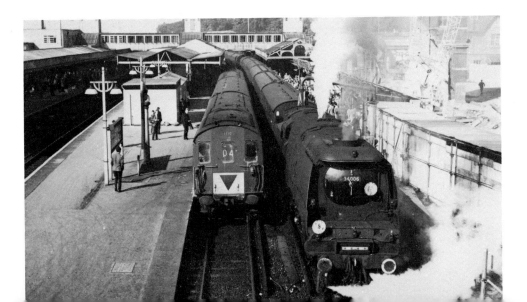

virtually as opened in 1895. The main buildings, of red brick with terra cotta embellishments, were on the up side. They were ornamented, in the same way as Nottingham Victoria and the LT stations of the 1930s, with an eye catching tower 100 ft high. The up platform was 600 ft long and the down, which had a bay road at its country end, was 800 ft. The signal cabin which adjoined the level crossing is just visible in the corner of the photograph. The up starting signal has co-acting arms, one for sighting above the footbridge and one below. Other details include the water crane, and the telegraph pole with its numerous crossbars. The fence on the left supports an array of enamelled advertisements.

The second view, taken in 1966, shows the effects of the rebuilding completed in 1935, with further work in progress. The 1930s rebuilding began with the replacement of the level crossing at the east end by a new road bridge at the west end. The massive reclamation scheme associated with the construction of the new docks made plenty of land available on the south side, so the down platform was converted to an island, and a new side platform with a bay was constructed on the down side. The number of platform roads, including the bay, was increased from 3 to 5. New buildings on what became the island platform, and on the down side, were constructed of concrete in the 'Odeon' style favoured by the Southern in the 1930s. A new bridge segregated passengers and parcels, with lifts for the parcels. During the Second World War the new buildings were badly damaged by bombs,

and still awaited repair 35 years later. Demolition of the 1895 buildings on the up side, including the tower, began in 1966, as shown in the photograph. It also shows two trains in platforms 1 and 2. Platform 2 is occupied by 3-H Unit No.1110 on a Portsmouth train. A relief to the northbound 'Pines Express' occupies platform 1, with London Midland Region coaches headed by unrebuilt West Country class No.34006 'Bude'. This was built at Brighton works in 1945 and withdrawn in 1967. The locomotive is taking water, while steam escapes from both safety valves and cylinder cocks, and the blast is turned on.

The third view shows the somewhat austere block, erected by developers, which contains office accommodation as well as the usual station facilities. It was opened in 1967, and so Southampton continues to show the chronological assymmetry which it has displayed since 1935 – that is, having one side of the station different in date and style from the other. Detailed changes include the new lamp posts, the station name boards, and the removal of the water cranes. The live rail appears in both views, but in 1966 it was unused and not yet provided with a wooden guard. The train in platform 2 is a stopping train from Bournemouth to Waterloo, consisting of 4 VEP Set No.7807, built at York in 1970. The up Weymouth express in platform 1 consists of 2 4-TC units hauled by 4-REP Unit No.3007, built at York in 1967. All that remains of the 1895 station is part of a platform face.

3 South East from London

70, 71 Swanley Junction, formerly LCDR (TQ 513684), on 24 December 1933 and 13 June 1959

The East Kent, later the London, Chatham and Dover Railway, was originally projected to fill an important gap in the SER, but for a variety of reasons became transformed into a rival main line. The route from Strood to Faversham was opened in 1858, by which time the line from London to Dover had been decided upon. The section from Strood to Bickley was opened in 1860. The branch to Sevenoaks was opened on 2 June 1862, and the station at the junction on 1 July 1862. It was named Sevenoaks Junction until 1871, when it was renamed Swanley Junction. The branch to Sevenoaks sprouted a further branch to Maidstone in 1874, and this was extended to Ashford in 1884. After the Union of the LCD and SER a few trains ran through to Dover by this route, but it was under Southern Railway management that it was upgraded to become a third route for boat trains to Dover. With electrification to Maidstone and the Medway towns it was decided that fast trains would be divided or joined at Swanley, consisting of Gillingham and Maidstone sections. The junction station was beyond the junction, and so a new Swanley was opened in 1939, west of the point of divergence.

Both views show the old station, the first being taken from the down main line platform on the Christmas Eve of 1933. The arrangement of the platforms was a common one for a branch line, as it enabled a train to wait in the branch platforms without obstructing the main line. The buildings were in the vee between the two lines, and as the site had to be excavated, it was somewhat restricted. Location in a cutting presented drainage problems and the down main platform was provided with a central drainage channel to prevent water running onto the tracks. Water cranes were provided, that on the up branch line being partly obscured by the locomotive. Track details included the fouling bars at the approach to the crossing. Lower

quadrant signals were provided, the sighting for the up starter being improved by the use of a bracket post and the cutting away of part of the valance on the station canopy. The branch starter has co-acting arms for visibility both above and below the footbridge, the need for a tall post arising because the approach from the branch is on a curve. Both posts carry the white lozenge indicating exemption from Rule 55. The train is from Maidstone East, hauled by 0-6-0 C Class locomotive No.1575. This was built at Ashford Works in 1903 and withdrawn in 1961.

The second view was taken from a steam-hauled down Kent Coast express on the last day of steam operation on the main line. The footbridge and parts of the platforms have been removed. The track layout was modified, with four tracks running west into the new Swanley Station, which had four platform roads. Live rail has been added and of the two diamond crossings, one is fixed and one moveable. The extra space required was obtained by removing some of the bank and increasing the angle of slope by means of a brick retaining wall. Electric point motors and colour lights replaced manual signalling. One survival is the water tank, obscured by the footbridge in the first view. The train in the siding consists of 1496 class set No.S4330. This was originally No.1500 built in 1926 for the Southern's Eastern Section electrification. It consisted of two driving motor coaches built by the Metropolitan Carriage, Wagon and Finance Co. and a trailer by the Birmingham Railway Carriage and Wagon Co. In 1946 a second trailer coach, built at Eastleigh, was added and the set was renumbered 4330. One of the motor coaches, and the original trailer appear in the photograph. Since this photograph was taken, the buildings of Swanley Junction have been demolished, and evidence of its existence becomes increasingly sparse.

72, 73 Chatham Station, formerly LCDR (TQ 755677), on 13 June 1959 and 11 November 1971

As mentioned just now, the line from Strood to Faversham was opened in 1858, and Chatham Station was opened at the same time. It was squeezed into the stretch of line between Fort Pitt and Chatham Tunnels. The site was crossed by two thoroughfares – Maidstone Road and Railway Street – and buildings were erected behind a small forecourt on Railway Street bridge. Because of the restricted site, goods traffic was handled at a separate goods depot, near Rochester Station; passengers however, including the armed services, have always been plentiful, especially since the electrification of the line to London in 1939.

The first view was taken on the last day of steam to the Kent Coast in 1959. Rebuilding is in progress but the previous layout is still apparent. Chatham consisted of two island platforms with a private siding serving Messrs Fyffes on the down side. Also on the down side was a short platform used principally for mail and forces traffic. On the up side were the facilities for horse and carriage traffic, including any end loading bay with a loading gauge. The long side platform was mainly used for the special traffic of the Army and Navy. Chatham was a decidedly dark

station, especially in the area below Railway Street, into which one descended from the booking hall. Rebuilding included the provision of better lighting, and new buildings at platform level.

The second view was taken in 1971 from a point slightly to one side of the 1959 photograph. The platforms have been extended and converted from island to side platforms; the new lamp posts are visible. As indicated by the concentration of 'Brute' trolleys on the up platform, mail and parcels traffic is still heavy. The small platform on the down side is occupied by a parcels van. Roof styles indicate the position of the new buildings at platform level. A significant change is the replacement of the area devoted to the Horse and Carriage Traffic by a car park. The train consists of 4-EPB Set No. 5355 built at Eastleigh in 1960. It was forming the 14.26 from Gillingham to Charing Cross via the Bexleyheath line. Chatham was always a very distinctive station but with little architectural merit. Even with the departure of gas light, steam and traditional signalling, together with the new buildings, it still falls comfortably short of the BR modern image.

74, 75 Sheerness-on-Sea Station, formerly LCDR (TQ 918748), on 15 June 1957 and 15 July 1972

When the LCD opened their Strood to Faversham line in 1858, the Isle of Sheppey, with its naval dockyard at Sheerness, was an obvious candidate for a branch line. This was opened by a nominally independent company in 1860, but was always operated by the LCDR. To serve commercial steamer services a spur was opened to a pier at Queenborough in 1876. The original terminal adjoined the dockyard, and in 1883 a short branch was constructed to a new station located in the residential part of Sheerness. This was something of a counterblast to the ferry service to Sheerness provided by the SER from their new pier at Port Victoria. Holiday traffic was encouraged by naming the new station Sheerness-on-Sea, while the first station was re-named Sheerness Dockyard. Most trains reversed in the Dockyard station to run on to Sheerness-on-Sea.

After the outbreak of war in December 1914 Sheerness-on-Sea was closed, and did not re-open until January 1922. At the same time the original station was closed to passengers, and a spur was opened to enable trains to run direct into Sheerness-on-Sea without reversal. In 1959 the Sheerness branch was electrified and the section on the mainland doubled. However, the island section remained single and is one of the few single track branch lines to achieve electrification. All the signal boxes have been closed, and the branch is controlled from the power box at Sittingbourne. In 1977 Sheerness was well served with an off-peak service of two trains an hour.

The first view shows the modest, weather-boarded

buildings of 1883. There was no question of extension, so they were built across the end of the tracks. No station master's house was provided and the total effect was hardly prestigious, especially if the station was intended to attract traffic from the rival SE route via Port Victoria. The booking office windows may be distinguished by their protective iron bars. Part of the valance of the canopy has been sawn away to improve the lighting. This may account for the abbreviated form in which the station name appears on the canopy, or it may be that there seemed to be no point in telling people already in Sheerness that the sea was available. Although the photograph was taken nine years after nationalisation, the name British Railways does not appear, both the poster boards and the station name board still being marked for the Southern Railway.

In February 1971 a train failed to stop, and demolished a considerable part of the station. The view taken in 1972 shows the surviving half, with new buildings under construction on the site of the other half. The weather-boarded walls, slate roof and brick chimney remain but none of the poster boards. The only board fixed to the building is headed 'Diary of Events', and is blank. The portable boards for newspapers reveal inconsistencies, such as that headed 'News of the World', which carries a query from the Daily Mirror – 'Has Britain's Beer Gone Off?' The station name board however now carries the full title of the station.

76, 77 Leysdown Station, formerly LCDR (TR 033708), on 2 December 1950 and 7 June 1954

The Sheppey Light Railway was promoted in the hope that it would stimulate the growth of a major seaside resort at Leysdown. With the advantage of hindsight, Leysdown appears as an unlikely starter, but when the line from Queenborough was opened in 1901 the SECR were sufficiently impressed to lease it. Later, in 1905, they purchased it. This led to a slightly unusual situation. The engineer of this light railway was Mr (later Lt-Colonel) H.F. Stephens, and all the stations were of corrugated iron, possessing a strong affinity to those on the Rother Valley. However, takeover by a main line company resulted in upgraded track, concrete replacing old sleepers for platform faces, and a general conformity to normal branch line standards. There always seemed to be hope of imminent development. A large estate was laid out at Leysdown and a Marine Parade constructed, but most of the plots remained empty. After the war a hotel for 1200 guests was hopefully projected, but nothing materialised. In 1939 Southern Railway officials visited Leysdown, and finding many campers on the foreshore, decided to investigate the possibility of following the precedent of the LMSR at Rhyl, and setting up a holiday camp. After the end of the Second World War, the RAF station which had been opened on the line at Eastchurch during the First World War became an open Borstal, and this had little demand for rail service. It was clear that Leysdown was not going to support a railway, and the Sheppey Light Railway was closed in December 1950.

The first view records the scene on the last day, 2 December 1950, after the arrival of the 10.55 train from Queenborough. It consisted of a two-coach articulated set and a 4-wheel parcels van. The articulated set was made up from the bodies of SER steam rail cars Nos.1 and 2,

resurrected as 2-coach set No.514. Rail Car No.1 had operated on the Sheppey Light Railway when it was first delivered in 1905. The locomotive, No.31705, which had run round its train shortly before the picture was taken, was an 0-4-4T of the R1 class. It was built by Sharp, Stewart in 1900 and was withdrawn in 1951. In fact the locomotive was 9 months older than the Sheppey Light Railway. There were no signals on the Sheppey by 1950; the turnouts to the goods sidings were operated by ground frames. By the last day the goods yard at Leysdown had been cleared and, in the photograph, is occupied by railway enthusiasts. Unfortunately the Colonel-Stephens-type corrugated iron station is obscured by the train. The buildings around the station give a fairly faithful impression of Leysdown in 1950. The structure with the striped roof, beyond the cattle pens, was a Dodgem Car arena which only came to life in summer. Most of the shack-like buildings were weekend residences, which were also somewhat lifeless in December.

It cannot be claimed that the closure of the railway had much impact on Leysdown, the characteristic form of transport for visitors and weekend residents being mature motor cars or motor cycle combinations. The second view shows the site three and a half years after closure, by which time the tracks had been removed and the station buildings removed. Evidence of the railway lingered in the strip of track ballast, in the hump marking the site of the cattle pen and, in particular, in the concrete-faced platform. It was however only a matter of time before the site was levelled for use as a car and coach park. There is no doubt that the Sheppey Light Railway served the Isle of Sheppey, but it can have given little satisfaction to railway shareholders.

78, 79 Approach to Dover Marine Station, formerly SECR (TR 320402), in 1921 and on 20 May 1961

The SE reached their Dover terminal, later named Dover Town Station, in 1844. There were grand plans for an impressive station designed by Lewis Cubitt but this was never completed, and the unspent capital was diverted to the construction of the Lord Warden Hotel, opened in 1851. This coincided with the use by cross-channel steamers of the nearby Admiralty Pier. Passengers had to make their own way from the station to the pier until, in 1861, the railway was extended alongside the steamers. Three years later the LCD opened a corresponding extension from their Dover Harbour and Town Station. The pier proved increasingly inadequate, and new facilities were opened for military traffic only in 1914. $11\frac{3}{4}$ acres were reclaimed on the leeward side of the pier, on which the SECR built their new Marine Station. It remains one of the most elaborate of marine terminals, comparing favourably with those at Weymouth, Southampton or Fishguard. The two island platforms, about 700 ft long by 60 ft wide, carried buildings devoted to the convenience of passengers. The Marine Station was opened for public services in January 1919, and the SECR selected it for the site of the war memorial to the 556 of their people who had been killed. Electric services reached Dover Marine from London via Chatham in 1959 and via Tonbridge or Maidstone in 1961.

Dover Marine, being in an exposed position, was subject to high winds; because of the wind tunnel effect of its overall roof, walls were built at both ends with openings for the tracks. Both views were taken from outside the end wall, but at the time of the electrification the two island platforms were extended outside the walls, so the second view (from the platform end) is rather nearer to the Lord Warden Hotel. The island platforms were unusually wide, so that there are wide gaps between the two central tracks and those on either side. The western island is numbered 5 and 6, and the eastern 3 and 4. (1 and 2 roads are outside the building.) Both views are taken from the end of platform 5, with trains running into platform 3. At the time of the first view there were only single track connections to the Town and to the Harbour stations. The Dover Marine Signal Box, which is contemporary with the station, is visible behind the pilot locomotive. The long footbridge provided access for guests at the hotel and also for passengers arriving on foot. Of the four coaches of the train in the photograph, a SECR brake with birdcage lookout is leading, followed by three Pullman cars. The pilot locomotive No.458 belongs to Stirling's B class, was built for the SE by Neilson Reid in 1898 and withdrawn in 1931. The train locomotive, No.497, was built as a Wainwright E class at Ashford Works in 1907. It was rebuilt to E1 class by Beyer, Peacock in 1920 and was withdrawn in 1960. Both locomotives are in SECR livery with plates bearing the company's initials on the cab sides,

and their numbers on the tenders.

The second view shows the scene about forty years later. The Lord Warden survives as office accommodation, having been closed as a hotel during the war. A new, covered footbridge has been added for passengers not arriving by train, and joins on to that shown in the first view. Both lines have been doubled and there is now access from the former LCD to platform 6. There is still a lavish provision of check rails on the sharp curves, but they are provided only on the inner rail, and not on both as in 1921. The live rails are conspicuous, together with wooden guards. The train is hauled by a Class 71 electric locomotive No.E5013, later No.71013. This was built at Doncaster Works in 1959. The pantograph was provided for working on sidings equipped with overhead wires. The luggage van is followed by a standard Mark 1 coach. By 1977 the post war boom in rail and sea cross-channel traffic had ended, eroded by aeroplanes and roll-on roll-off ferries. The best known of the boat trains, the 'Golden Arrow', was reduced to combination with another train before its withdrawal in 1972. After a prolonged exclusion of passengers not using steamers, a reflection of the decline of boat train traffic is witnessed by the advent of a normal hourly service of trains from Dover Marine.

80, 81, 82 Hythe Station, formerly SER (TR 167354), in 1921, on 1 August 1954 and 18 April 1969

The branch of the SE main line from Sandling Junction to Sandgate was opened in 1874. Ostensibly with the primary aim of serving the military establishment at Shorncliffe, the line had two other possibilities. First, it was intended to develop Seabrook, near Sandgate, as a resort, and the SE opened the Imperial Hotel between Seabrook and Hythe. They also opened a horse tramway linking the centre of Hythe, the hotel, Sandgate Station and the town of Sandgate. Second, they obtained powers in 1876 to extend the line to Folkestone Harbour, but this costly extension, which, because of local opposition, would have been largely in tunnel, was never constructed. It was however this possibility that explains the provision of double track on a lightly used line. By 1931 mechanised road transport was taking passengers direct to main line stations, so the line from Sandling to the intermediate station at Hythe was made single, and the rest of the branch was abandoned. During the Second World War what had become the Hythe branch closed from 1943 until 1945. Finally, in 1951, it closed permanently, being replaced by a bus service to the main line at Sandling.

Hythe Station was sited well above the town, with weather-boarded buildings of the type frequently constructed in the later part of the Victorian period. A rather free portrayal of the arrival of the first train in 1874 indicates that, apart from some extension and heightening of the platforms, there were no major changes until the virtual abandonment of the down side after 1931. In particular the valance, which rather unusually surrounded all four sides of the waiting room, remained intact. In 1921 Hythe was fully signalled, but as the two SE lower quadrant signals in the photograph are both pulled off, and the possibility of two trains being due simultaneously is unlikely, it was probably not continuously manned. The signal cabin and the goods yard which adjoined the station are not shown. However, the station master's house with its two prominent gables arranged at right angles appears very clearly. Other details are the mile post, marking 67 miles from Charing Cross, the gas lamps and the wooden face of the down platform.

The 1954 view shows the station three years after closure. The tracks have been removed and vegetation is creeping over the site. The wooden buildings have gone, as well as the wooden platform face, but there can be no doubt of the identity of the site. If confirmation were needed, the underbridge beyond the station is in position, and one gable of the station master's house adjoins a tree. By 1969 the site had been flattened, but the station master's house remained to give an unambiguous fix. The brick pillars of the metal underbridge remained, but the bridge itself had gone for scrap. The intention was to use the site for building dwellings, and this would finally extinguish anything that might have remained of Hythe Station.

Hastings was a hybrid station, having three terminal platforms and one through, and also being served by both SE and LBSC trains. As far as the SE were concerned, Hastings could be approached either via Ashford or, more directly, via Tunbridge Wells. In fact when the station opened in 1851 the only railway available was the SE route of 93 miles from London Bridge via Redhill and Ashford. The LBSC route of $76\frac{1}{2}$ miles from London Bridge via Lewes was completed in 1851, and this included running powers over the SE into Hastings Station. However, one of the notorious railway 'battles' was staged, by which the LBSC trains were prevented from entering Hastings for some days. In 1852 the SE 'direct' line via Tunbridge Wells was opened, and the two companies agreed to pay their receipts, after the deduction of expenses, into a common pool, which was divided equally between them. For many years LBSC and SE express trains from London normally used the terminal, with trains from Ashford using the through platform. However in 1931 a new station with two through island platforms was opened. At the same time necessary improvements were made to the SE 'direct' line to enable Schools class locomotives to be used. This development favoured the SE route, but in 1935 the LBSC line received attention, with the introduction of electric trains. For operating convenience these did not terminate at Hastings but ran through to an electric train depot at Ore in suburban Hastings. Because of loading gauge restrictions it was not possible to use standard electric stock on the SE Hastings route, but in 1958 diesel electric trains were introduced. At the present time, 54 years after the LBSC and SE were joined in the Southern, their two routes for Hastings to London still co-exist.

The views down onto the old and the new stations were both taken from Linton Road overbridge to the west of the station. They are not well matched, the earlier view looking to the east – the ruins of the castle on the sky line give a fix – and the later roughly to the north east. The old station consisted essentially of two platforms in a vee, one side with a through line and one with a terminal. An island platform, visible to the right of the train, provided supplementary terminal facilities. Trains by the SE route retained Pullman cars until the demise of steam in 1958, and a Pullman car may be seen forming part of the train in the platform. Rolling stock in the siding adjoining the signal cabin appears to consist of coaches from the SE, the LCD and the LSW. The large goods shed is just visible over the top of the tree, but the SE engine shed is obscured, although an inspection pit appears in the foreground. The signal cabin, with its hipped roof and sash windows, is typical of the SE. None of the signals are sufficiently clear for detailed description, but there are SE-type bracketed signals at the end of each of the platforms.

Perhaps the best reference point for linking the two views is the top of the goods shed, which was not affected by the rebuilding of 1931 and may be seen over the footbridge which links the two island platforms with the station entrance. Another feature which appears in both views is the southern parapet of the Braybrooke Road underbridge, visible in the earlier view to the left of the signal cabin. In the 1974 photograph the site of the signal cabin and the siding appears as disused land. The sand trap is in roughly the same position as the inspection pit. Bracketed signals are provided at the end of each of the platforms. The 1930 signal cabin, of which the end gable is showing, appears to the left of the platforms. From an operating point of view, the new station was a great advance on its predecessor.

The views from the bridge give a general impression, but the third photograph was taken in 1929 from the west

end of the through platform, near the point of the vee. Characteristic SE features are the valance of the canopy and the station name board. The signal cabin on stilts with wagons underneath it is visible to the left, and the goods shed appears above the train. The platform surface appears to consist of small tiles, involving an amount of labour that would be unthinkable at the present day.

Track details include the trap on the siding adjoining the platform road. The train consists of LBSC coaches drawn by SECR L class locomotive No.A781, built by Borsig of Berlin in 1914 and withdrawn in 1959. Of all the features in the view, only the goods shed and the footbridge remain in 1976.

86, 87 Three Bridges Station, formerly LBSCR (TQ 288369), on 16 September 1963 and 16 July 1972

The main line to Brighton was completed in 1841, and Three Bridges, which served the neighbouring town of Crawley, was one of the original stations. It became a junction when the branch to Horsham was opened in 1848. This was extended to form part of the mid-Sussex route. On the opposite side of the line, the East Grinstead branch was completed in 1855 and later extended to Tunbridge Wells. The East Grinstead trains left from a bay platform on the down side. By 1900, the up platform had become an island, with its outer face frequently used by Horsham trains.

When the Brighton line was quadrupled from Earlswood to Three Bridges in 1907, a new island platform was added on the up side. The running lines were elevated, but the engine shed was originally built on the up side at ground level, so infilling was necessary for the new platform on the engine shed site. The displaced locomotives were housed in a new engine shed in the fork between the main and Horsham lines. The four track section was extended to Balcombe Tunnel in 1910. The Brighton main line was electrified throughout from the first day of 1933, but Three Bridges was the temporary terminus for electric trains from 17 July 1932. It was also the site of the control room for the 18 sub-stations between Purley, Brighton and Worthing. Colour lights replaced semaphore signals, and at Three Bridges the North and South signal boxes were closed, but the large cabin at the country end of the centre island platform was retained with a new lever frame. The line to East Grinstead was closed in 1968. The engine shed was closed in 1964, and a new signal cabin was constructed on the up side in 1952. With the development of Crawley New Town, traffic at Three Bridges increased to its present high level.

The two views show detailed changes. In 1963 the East Grinstead service was still operating, and Diesel-Electric 3-D Set No.1310 occupies the bay platform, forming the 12.08 departure. The overall roof, originally provided to form a carriage shed for the branch coaches at night, remained in position. The platforms had been raised to standard height in 1932 and the concrete platform face indicates an extension of the central platform. Although steam was very much on the decline, water cranes were provided on both platforms. The Southern type concrete lamp posts also carry the loudspeakers of the public address system. A traditional porter's trolley rests against a pillar of the overall roof. In addition to the roof, the three platform canopies are of interest, being of three different styles. That on the down main platform, projecting beyond the overall roof of the bay, is of considerable age, even if it is not original. The rather plain canopy on what has become the centre platform appears to be more recent, while that on the new island platform of 1908 has a typical LBSC valance of that period. The track is of the BR flat-bottomed variety, with a crossover in the foreground.

In the second view, the removal of the roof spanning the East Grinstead bay reveals the original station building of 1841. The water cranes have gone, and the lamp posts and station name boards have been replaced. Flat bottomed track is still in use, but the crossover has been moved to a point beyond the platforms. Somewhat surprisingly the water tank, visible above the island platform on the up side, survives. Three Bridges continues to offer a variety of period flavours, including the down side buildings of 1841 and the up side island platform of 1908.

88, 89 Lewes Station, formerly LBSCR (TQ 417098), on 15 March 1958 and 18 July 1972

The history of Lewes railway station is a complicated one. When it was opened in 1846 the line from Brighton ran into a terminus in Friar's Walk, and trains going beyond Lewes had to reverse in or out, as at Dorchester. However, there was a platform on the through line, and Lewes started to develop as a railway centre when in 1847 the direct route to the main line at Keymer, and the Newhaven branch, were opened. In 1857 a new station was opened at the junction of the lines from Keymer and Brighton, and the terminal closed after only eleven years of use (it was finally knocked down in 1967). A fifth line reached Lewes in 1858, this being the Uckfield branch,

later re-aligned and extended to Tunbridge Wells. Although the abandonment of the terminal facilitated operating, sharp reverse curves continued to impede traffic, and in 1884 powers were obtained to build a new line cutting off the original curve, which was retained for goods traffic. This necessitated the complete rebuilding of the passenger station and the new premises were opened in 1889. The East Sussex electrification of 1935 involved trains from Lewes in four directions – London, Brighton, Hastings and Newhaven – and only the Tunbridge Wells passenger trains remained steam hauled. In 1969 the Tonbridge route was closed south of Uckfield, after which

67

all the passenger services to Lewes were electrically worked. In the same year the goods depot was closed, and subsequently the original line through Lewes was lifted. The lavish provision of platforms was reduced by the closure of the down loop on the Brighton side in 1971, and that on the London side in 1972.

Lewes resembles the old Swanley Junction or the old Hastings in having its buildings in the vee between diverging platforms. Both views were taken from above the tunnel mouth, and show the London platforms, with the original line diverging to the left. The platforms are below street level, but the main building adjoins the road which can be seen crossing the platforms in the background. The station forecourt fronts an ample circulating area, surmounted by a roof with a lantern. This is a prominent feature towards the right of the photograph. The London side is shown with its three platform roads – up and down through, and down loop. As it carries freight only the old line is not electrified.

An unusual feature is the placing of the live rail on the down loop alongside the platform face near the turnout to the old line; this was necessitated by the position of the turnout. (Live rails were usually placed away from the platform, as on the through tracks.) The signal box controls the entry to the goods yard; level-crossing gates are visible beyond the overbridge. The ends of the two semaphore arms are visible on the left of the picture and three banner repeaters are mounted on the down island platform. Before 1935 the platforms ended a little beyond the banner repeater signals, but to take 12-car electric trains they were extended towards the tunnel mouth. The position of the junction precluded the possibility of extension at the other end. This in turn necessitated pushing the junction, with the old line, into the tunnel mouth. The canopy on the up side was lengthened, and the extension may be distinguished from the original roof of the LBSC. For instance the LBSC canopy is supported by pillars and the Southern's by brackets. Gas lamps are still in use; the post on the down platform also supports loud speakers.

The second view shows the scene after the lifting of the goods lines and the closure of the down loop. When the turnout between the down loop and the goods lines was removed the live rail was replaced, in its normal position, away from the platform face. The signal cabin still stands, but the point rodding and signal wires have been removed. Electric lighting has replaced gas, and includes a tall post from which a portion of the down platform is illuminated. The considerable expanse of canopy roof has been replaced by two 'bus stop' shelters. Simplification of the layout accounts for the removal of two of the banner repeater signals. The up express from Hastings and Eastbourne entering the platform is headed by 4-CIG Set No.7433. This was built at York in 1972. A number of Sussex country towns might compete for the greatest number of trains per hour per head of population; with a population of just over 14,000, Lewes had until recently 8 departures per hour – one to London, one to Eastbourne, one to Seaford, two to Ore and three to Brighton.

90, 91 Heathfield, formerly LBSC (TQ 581203), on 4 April 1959 and 4 October 1973

Heathfield was opened in 1880 on the line from Tunbridge Wells to Eastbourne. The earliest part of the route was the branch from Polegate, on the Hastings line, to the market town of Hailsham, opened in 1849. The Brighton to Tunbridge Wells route was completed by the line between Uckfield and Groombridge, opened in 1868. In 1873 a nominally independent company, the Tunbridge Wells and Eastbourne Railway, was authorised to join the Uckfield line near Rotherfield to Hailsham. Protracted negotiations ended with an agreement for the LBSC to construct and operate the line, but with SERs running powers to Eastbourne. A new Act of 1876 altered the alignment and required stations to be provided at Rotherfield, Mayfield, Cross-in-Hand (for Heathfield), Horeham and Hellingly. The SE exercised their running powers, and from April 1884 until December 1885 ran an express from Charing Cross to Eastbourne. This was not a success, and subsequently the SE confined itself to collecting a small share of the Eastbourne revenue – in effect, as protection money. A few trains ran through between Victoria and Eastbourne, but the basic service through Heathfield was always between Tunbridge Wells and Eastbourne. The passenger service ended in 1965, but Heathfield kept its goods service via Hailsham until 1968.

As will be seen from the first view, Heathfield was a two level station, with solid red brick buildings at street level and wooden waiting accommodation on each of the platforms. The booking office was in the main station house, and passengers reached the up side by means of the public road over the bridge and a ramp down to the platform; the down platform was reached by a flight of wooden steps. Heathfield was a passing place on this single line route, and originally had signal boxes at each end, but latterly that at the London end was downgraded from block post to ground frame. The substantial goods shed and the platform for horse and carriage traffic appears on the right of the photograph. When the letters forming the word Heathfield were removed for the invasion emergency of 1940 they must have been mislaid, as only a small name plate has been affixed to the station name board. Chaired track is in use with concrete sighting marks for checking the alignment of the curve. The platform coping is formed of bricks and the surface of gravel. The gas lamps are of special interest as for many years Heathfield had its own gas supply. Natural gas was discovered by accident when a borehole was put down to provide the station with water, and this was used for lighting and, until 1930, to operate a small gas engine for pumping water. The down train of BR Mark I coaches is waiting to pass an up train, and is hauled by BR 2-6-4T No.80016. This was built at Brighton Works in 1951 and withdrawn in 1967.

The second view is largely negative in character, showing the state of Heathfield eight years after trains ceased to call. All the tracks have been removed and the platforms cleared. The station house however is still lived in; Heathfield presents an aspect of the railway scene common in the 1970s.

92, 93 Rye Station, Rye and Camber Tramway, (TQ 925206), about 1935 and on 24 March 1967

Like the Sheppey, the Rye and Camber was designed by Col Stephens, but did not come to form part of his 'empire'. It was opened, from a terminal on the outskirts of Rye to Rye Harbour 1½ miles away, in 1895. It was extended for a further ½ mile to Camber Sands in 1908 when Rye Harbour Station was re-named Golf Links. This 3 ft gauge line was isolated, and modest in every respect. Its total locomotive stock amounted to 2, but in 1925 it purchased an internal combustion machine, resembling a rail mounted lawn mower. On the strength of this it sold one locomotive in 1926 and the second in 1937. Two years later, with the outbreak of war, the Rye and Camber

was closed, and has never re-opened. There were no earthworks so it provides an excellent example of a line which has disappeared, almost without a trace.

The first view shows the terminal at Rye. No rolling stock is in sight, so presumably the train had gone to Camber. The impression is of an unconventional establishment, and indeed in many details the Rye and Camber diverged from normal railway practice. To start with the track gauge was 3 ft, and the flat-bottomed rails rested on sleepers which were buried in the gravel ballast. Points were actuated by weighted levers, an example appearing in the foreground of the photograph. The boundary fence was made of iron railings of the type usually found on gentlemen's estates. In fact, iron was also the material from which most of the buildings were constructed. The engine shed is on the left of the passenger platform. The station building is clearly related to those of the Sheppey or the southern section of the Kent and East Sussex, and has the unmistakable imprint of Colonel H.F.

Stephens. Although not visible on the photograph, the words 'Tram Station' were painted on the roof in the hope of attracting visitors seeing it from the ramparts of the hill town. As the Rye and Camber lacked a number of the features which the Board of Trade expected of a railway, the use of the word 'tram' may have been a cunning device. Among other things, as shown in the photograph, there were no signals. As there was never more than one locomotive in use the lack was not a serious one, and the line was commendably free from accidents.

The second view indicates a maximum degree of change, Rye Station having disappeared without trace. A fix is provided by the house on the right and the bridge over the river in the background. It is possible that aerial photography might show something not visible from ground level, but there is little to indicate that this is the site from which, between 1895 and 1939, thousands of people departed for the pleasures of the golf links or of Camber Sands.

94, 95 Bognor Station, formerly LBSCR (SZ 933994), about 1906 and on 5 August 1974

When the LBSC West Coast line was opened in 1846, a station named Bognor was opened about 3½ miles away from the resort. The name was hurriedly changed to Woodgate, and then, from 1847 until 1853, back to Bognor. Finally from 1853 until its closure in 1864, it reverted to Woodgate for Bognor. It was closed in 1864 because the branch line to Bognor was opened. The first

terminus was not only decidedly simple but, in 1897, had its roof blown off. This was repaired, and then in 1899, fortunately at the end of the season, it was burned down. Temporary buildings were hastily erected, but by 1902 the present station was complete, an excellent example of an Edwardian seaside station. Bognor grew both in size and popularity when King George V selected it for convalescence, and in 1929, when the town changed its name to Bognor Regis, the railway station followed suit. The branch was electrified in 1938, and has for many years had through services to London. If the site of Rye Station provided an example of maximum change, Bognor exemplified minimal change, as the two views demonstrate.

The first view was taken not long after the opening of the station, with everybody in sight intent on the heavy camera on its tripod. The porter has paused, with the boater-hatted owner of the box on his trolley looking on. The patrons of the bookstall are gazing in different directions, and further in the background are the inevitable small boys. The concourse is extensive and, with the glazing in the roof, well lit. The refreshment room projects onto the concourses, its curved roof bringing it to the attention of passengers. On the left the handrails of a passenger weighing machine are visible. Doors are marked 'Telegraph Office' and 'Station Master'. Wooden barriers regulate access to the trains. The station and the people belong very much to their period.

The second photograph, taken about 68 years later with a small camera and 1/500th of a second exposure, shows only changes of detail. The bookstall is still in the same place, albeit with larger premises. The roof of the Refreshment Room is visible, but if the weighing machine is still there, it is obscured by the 'Brute' trolley. This represents a development from the porter's trolley in the first view. The basic structure remains unchanged and, being well lit and spacious, there is no reason why it should not. The notices, on the other hand, might well have puzzled Edwardian travellers – especially 'Self-help luggage trolleys'. Electric lights have replaced gas, and some new features catch the eye; in particular, loud speakers, a litter bin and circular seats do not appear on the Edwardian station. But these are details and, on balance, Bognor presents an outstanding example of the unchanging railway scene.

4 North East from London

96, 97, 98 Ongar, formerly Great Eastern Railway (TL 551035), on 11 June 1938, in 1956 and on 14 December 1963

The impecunious Eastern Counties Railway hopefully projected lines into rural Essex, their branch to Loughton being opened in 1856. By the time the extension of $11\frac{1}{4}$ miles to the small market town of Ongar was completed in 1865, the ECR had been merged into the Great Eastern; no industries arose to swell the traffic, and double track has never stretched beyond Epping. However, under the London Transport New Works Programme of 1935–1940, passenger services on the branch were to be taken over by London Transport. War delayed the completion of electrification, and it was September 1949 when Central Line tube trains at last reached Epping. There followed a period of suspense, with the end section of the line being worked with a shuttle service of British Railway steam trains using vintage Great Eastern locomotives. Finally, on 16 November 1957, LT took the plunge, and tube trains began to operate the shuttle service between Epping and Ongar. It is probably the nearest approach to the Metropolitan's rural Brill branch to be found on London Transport today.

The first view shows Ongar in LNER days. The station consisted of one side platform with substantial brick buildings towards the inner end. There was no canopy and few seats, but patches of garden relieved the expanse of platform. Instead of freestanding posts, the gas lamps had short posts mounted on a wall. One corner of the small engine shed is visible, with No.7147 alongside the ashes removed from the fireboxes of locomotives. No.7147 was built at the Stratford Works of the GER in 1903, and belonged to the LNER F5 class. The locomotive on the three-coach train at the platform was No.7144, also built at Stratford in 1903, classified F5 by the LNER and withdrawn by British Railways in 1955.

When the second view was taken in 1956, London

Transport had taken over the line but BR provided the locomotives and rolling stock. By this time, No.7147 had become No.67193; during the war, the top of the chimney was removed to permit running over the Metropolitan and the District underground lines of London Transport. Thirty-six engines treated in this way would have worked on the Underground if key power stations had been damaged. Five locomotives were prepared by BR in 1949 to be kept at Epping to work the passenger service between Epping and Ongar. The trains consisted of two-coach sets of LNER compartment stock, fitted for push-pull working.

The equipment was vacuum operated, and part of it is visible attached to the side of smokebox of the locomotive. For freight and other workings over the electrified line from Epping to Leyton the locomotives were fitted with trip-cocks, which made automatic brake applications if a signal was passed at danger. By 1956 the engine shed had been demolished, but the top of the water tank may be seen over the leading coach. The signal box, with GER lower quadrant starting signal, was still operational. In November 1957 electric tube trains took over, and the locomotives, including No.67193, were withdrawn.

By the time the third view was taken from the Signal Box steps in 1963, electric operation was well established. Electric lamps had replaced gas, and the traditional signalling had given way to colour light – the back of a signal is visible on the platform. However, many facilities lingered, such as the platform for horse and carriage traffic or livestock, and the goods shed. Coal wagons appear to the left of the goods shed. Ongar was finally closed to freight in 1966, and subsequently the sidings were removed, but the passenger station remains, at the end of London Transport's most rural single line railway.

73

99 Viaduct near Witham, formerly Great Eastern Railway (TL 826139), on 30 June 1958

The Maldon, Witham and Braintree Railway, linking the port of Maldon to the inland towns of Witham and Braintree, was authorised in 1846. It was absorbed, with the aid of some doubtful promises, by the Eastern Counties Railway and opened in 1848. Apart from the prestigious terminal at Maldon, the line was built without extravagance, including the use of timber where this was cheaper than brickwork. It was planned to cross the EC main line on the level at Witham, but spurs were provided into the EC station, and the MWB was normally worked as two separate branches from Witham, as opposed to the original idea of feeding traffic through the port of Maldon. The two sections were not equally successful, and the Maldon branch was finally closed in 1966.

A wooden viaduct east of Witham remained in use until the closure of the line, and in its latter days was a rarity on British Railways. The branch train, on its way back from Maldon to Witham, consists of ex-GER and ex-LNER corridor coaches, hauled by a class J15 0-6-0 freight locomotive running tender first.

100, 101, 102 Maldon Station, formerly GER (TL 853076), about 1908, on 25 May 1970 and 20 January 1977

Maldon. East Station.

Perhaps more than other railway companies, those in East Anglia spent considerable sums on impressive stations. In the case of Maldon there is a story, possibly apocryphal, that the splendour of the station owes something to the fact that David Waddington, deputy Chairman of the Eastern Counties, was Tory candidate for the constituency. In any event, there can be no doubt about the architectural merit of the magnificent edifice. It has the style of a Jacobean mansion, stressed by its ornate chimneys and Dutch gables. Across the front is a nine-arch arcade, reminiscent of the colonnade at Gosport. This is surmounted by a fine open-work parapet. Many of the details are noteworthy, including rainwater heads marked MWB and ECR. Behind all this, was a single platform, from which the passenger service was withdrawn in 1964.

The first view shows the station as it appeared during the Edwardian high summer of the railways. The peace of a sunny afternoon was little disturbed by the arrival of the

photographer, although one person did go as far as looking at him. The horse of the hotel bus has continued to gaze ahead.

The second view was taken on a dull afternoon in May 1970, about 6 years after closure to passengers. The gates to the station yard had gone and entry was free to vandals and those with less destructive inclinations alike. A certain amount of boarding up of windows had taken place, but any unprotected glass was shattered. The wall letter box, located under the centre arch, had been removed. Despite careful maintenance until closure, the future of the building was doubtful.

By the January of 1977 all had changed. The forecourt was again closed, and new windows had replaced the mixture of board and broken glass which filled the casements in 1970. The prestigious terminal of the Maldon, Witham and Braintree Railway was to survive by virtue of being opened as a restaurant.

103, 104, 105, 106 White Notley Station, formerly GER (TL 788187), on 30 June 1958, 20 January 1977, about 1900 and 20 January 1977

As mentioned already, the Maldon, Witham and Braintree Railway was opened in 1848. Inevitably there was a public demand for stations from a number of points on the line. Long before the advent of halts modest establishments were occasionally opened, often adjoining level crossings, which were not stations by normal Victorian standards. They had no goods facilities, no station house and offices, and sometimes did not issue tickets. White Notley conforms to this description except for the issue of tickets. The Braintree line was built with double track, but was made single during the Crimean War, so White Notley could have incorporated a passing place. However, as the first view shows, there were no facilities for crossing

trains, and the signal box, despite its appearance, had for many years done no more than operate the crossing gates, with their protecting signals. The signals are not visible in either the first or second photographs, but the wooden posts supporting pulleys and wire can be seen on the right of the track. The first photograph was taken in 1958, when there had been no great changes since the Victorian period. The brick shelter with its canopy, and the wooden waiting room and office belonged to the same period as the oil lamp. The branch train approaching the crossing was hauled by No.65465, a J15 class 0-6-0 built by the GER at Stratford Works in 1912 and withdrawn in 1962. The Second World War pillboxes, visible in the 1977 view,

WHITE NOTLEY. 1713.

Fred Spalding.
Photo
Chelmsford.
Copyright.

were concealed by the buildings on the platform.

The second photograph shows the scene during the electrification of the Braintree branch. The things unchanged are the track, the signal box, the crossing gates and the wire leading to the signal. The bricks and flagstones of the platform have been replaced by concrete blocks and blacktop, and the level has been raised. Both the original buildings have been demolished and replaced by a pre-fabricated shelter of metal and glass. Electric lights have been provided instead of oil lamps. Of particular significance are the posts placed alongside the track in preparation for electrification.

The third and fourth photographs indicate the changes

between 1900 and 1977 to be seen from the east side of the level crossing. Perhaps the most remarkable feature is the almost complete lack of change in the signal box, the crossing gates and the adjoining fences. Even the platform provided outside the signal box for window cleaning has not been provided with a handrail. The adjacent house has undergone rather more changes, including the replacement of the roof tiles. The semaphore signal with its prominent finial, together with the adjacent enamelled advertisements, has been removed. However, the most remarkable development is the imminence of electrification, due in October 1977, on a single line branch in Essex.

107, 108 Colchester Station, formerly GER (TL 992264), on 13 October 1957 and 20 January 1977

In 1843 the Eastern Counties Railway Company managed to open its line from London as far as Colchester and there, as a result of financial exhaustion, construction ceased. The modest station was joined by a lavish hotel financed by Samuel Moreton Peto. When it became clear that the Eastern Counties could go no further, the Eastern Union were authorised to construct a line between Colchester and Ipswich. The approach to the Eastern Counties terminus was on a sharp curve, and this became significant in 1846 when the Eastern Union made an end-on junction with the Eastern Counties. Colchester became a through station instead of a terminus, with a rigid speed limit applied to its western approaches. Over the years improvements were made, notably in 1865 and 1894, but major changes, including the elimination of the curve, did not take place until 1962. The new alignment cut across the old curve, and an extension to the up platform followed it. Work was begun before the War, came to a halt, and was not resumed until the end of the 1950s.

The first view was taken from the new platform extension looking to the east in 1957. The original alignment, with its 40 mph speed restriction, may be seen on the extreme left. What was to become the new main line, on the left of the platform, was being used as a siding

holding BR, LMS, GE and LNE coaching stock. Lamp posts were in position, but as the platform was not in use, they were not provided with lamps. Electric point motors and boards for sealing corridor connections lay in the foreground. Colchester Station signal box, shored up with baulks of timber, is visible to the left of the new canopy. From left to right the skyline includes a water tank, a telegraph post, a cylindrical water softening tower, a bracketed semaphore signal with the original water tank beyond it and, appearing faintly on the extreme right, the tower of Peto's hotel – which became a mental hospital.

The second view was taken late on the afternoon of 20 January 1977. The new platform was in use with concrete lamp posts and strip lighting already turned on. The most obvious change is the overhead electric wiring. The line from Colchester to Clacton was electrified in 1959, but until 1962 there was a non-electrified gap between Chelmsford and Colchester. The full electric service from Liverpool Street to Clacton via Colchester was introduced in 1963. The new alignment, together with a signal box with colour-light signals and the new length of platform, was brought into use in 1962. The water softening plant had gone, but the tower of Peto's ill-fated hotel was still visible on the skyline.

109, 110 Approach to Norwich Thorpe Station, formerly GER (TQ 244080), on 19 September 1954 and 7 August 1958

There has been a station at Norwich Thorpe since the opening of the line to Yarmouth in 1844. A number of companies were involved in the construction of the first route to London which was opened via Ely and Cambridge in 1845, but from 1848 it was operated throughout by the Eastern Counties Railway. Its monopoly of Norwich traffic was broken in 1849, when the Eastern Union completed their route from an end-on junction with the Eastern Counties at Colchester to a second terminal – Norwich Victoria. A spur of 1851 gave trains from the Eastern Union access to Norwich Thorpe and, especially after 1854 when the EU was taken over by the Eastern Counties, Thorpe became the principal Norwich terminal. Its importance was recognised by the erection of the present impressive buildings in 1886. Norwich Victoria was closed to passenger traffic in 1916.

The two views were taken from the Carrow Road bridge looking towards the station, the dome of which appears on the skyline on the right. Both views show the engine sheds on the left. The large concrete coaling plant is visible in the 1954 view but obscured by smoke in that of 1958. This was erected in 1935 and demolished in 1962. The tracks running ahead, past the engine sheds, led to the goods depot and to the site of the first Thorpe Station. The lines curving to the right serve the present station, opened in 1886. In 1954 steam was still unchallenged, and the haze of smoke drifting over from the engine sheds slightly

obscures the skyline. The signal controlling running into the station is Great Eastern in style, with lower quadrant arms and one of the posts surmounted by a finial.

The main change by 1958 was the construction of the fuelling point for diesel locomotives and trains, constructed in space available in the right foreground. Locomotive No.D5513 (now No.31013 of Class 31), delivered new from Brush in 1958, is taking fuel. At this time however, steam was still in evidence and Class J50/2 No.68905 is to be seen propelling an empty train into the platforms. This was constructed for the GNR at their Doncaster Works in 1915 and was withdrawn in 1960. The coach next to the engine is of LNER design but the remainder are BR Mark 1. Most of the coaches are in plum and spilt milk livery but at least two are painted in the maroon which replaced it. Traffic was still controlled by the signal box visible in the centre of both photographs, but the bracket signals of 1954 had been removed. The new main departure signal, with metal posts and upper quadrant arms, occupied roughly the same position as the previous home signal. A fogman's hut is visible just beyond it. However, the signals on the goods line remained unchanged. Dieselization has now been complete for many years but, apart from the demise of the steam running sheds, the view from Carrow Road bridge has changed very little.

111, 112, 113 Stoke Ferry Station, formerly GER (TL 707997), about 1900, on 24 July 1955 and 21 January 1977

The branch from the main line to King's Lynn at Denver to the small town of Stoke Ferry was a typical Fenland branch. It ran for just over seven miles through a rich, agricultural area, virtually without earthworks or gradients. It was opened in 1882 and operated by the GER, who absorbed the original company in 1898. In 1906 a long branch was opened to serve farms to the south of the line, and in 1925 the Wissington Sugar Beet Factory was completed about a mile from its junction. Passenger service to Stoke Ferry ceased in 1930 but it remained open for goods traffic until 1965. The western end of the branch is still open to serve the sugar beet factory.

The first view shows a mixed train on arrival from Downham Market. Two GER coaches were hauled by a tank locomotive, with a characteristic stove-pipe chimney. A GER coach of perhaps even earlier date is visible on the left, re-roofed and with wheels removed, in use as an office. A loading-gauge marks the entrance to the goods yard, which was located off the picture, to the left. The signal box, and also a GER starting signal, project above the roof line of the train. The space under the platform canopy was lit by oil lamps.

The next view was taken on the occasion of the visit of the RCTS Fensman Rail Tour on a warm summer's day in 1955, about 25 years after closure to passengers. Freight traffic was still being handled in the goods yard on the left, with the lines serving the passenger platform being used as sidings. Both the station buildings and the railway houses to the right of the picture remained in use. The locomotive, Class J17 No.65562, was built at Stratford Works in 1905 and withdrawn in 1958. The signalling had been removed and, to enable the locomotive to run round its train of main line coaches, the points were being manually operated. The most striking change is the disappearance of the canopy from over the platform.

The third view was taken near the end of a cold winter afternoon early in 1977. The buildings were still inhabited but the railway tracks had been removed, and the site was in use as a repository for discarded road vehicles. As it was road vehicles that led to the closure of Stoke Ferry Station, it is perhaps not inappropriate that it should provide a graveyard for some of them.

114, 115, 116, 117 Lines west of Barking, formerly LTSR (TQ 440846), on 16 February 1957, 24 August 1957, 7 June 1958 and 18 June 1976

The London, Tilbury and Southend Railway was opened from a junction with the Eastern Counties near Forest Gate, to Tilbury for Gravesend, in 1854, and on to Southend in 1856. A cut-off line from a point west of Barking to Gas Factory Junction, opened in 1858, gave access to the Fenchurch Street terminus, saving distance and avoiding the danger of delays at Stratford. Initially the LTS was operated by contractors, but in 1875 it assumed responsibility for its own running; this was followed by a spate of development, including the completion in 1888 of the cut-off line from Barking to Pitsea via Upminster. In 1894 a connection between Tottenham and Forest Gate gave access to the St Pancras terminal of the Midland Railway. Finally, in 1908, an extension of the Metropolitan District line from Whitechapel brought that company's electric trains into Barking. The LTS was absorbed by the Midland in 1912, passed to the LMSR in 1923, and to British Railways in 1948.

Traffic approaches Barking from the west from the LTS main line to Fenchurch Street, from the District and Metropolitan lines of London Transport, and from the rest of the British Railways system via Forest Gate. To the east the lines via Upminster and Tilbury diverge, and London Transport trains follow independent tracks to Upminster. In connection with the electrification of the LTS it was decided to construct complex junctions, involving flyovers to the west of Barking and a burrowing crossover to the east. The four views all looking to the west show the changing scene from Tanner Street footbridge, which is situated about quarter of a mile to the west of the station. The first view shows an early stage in the construction work. Basically, this consisted of two flyovers, the first of which carried the lines from the Forest Gate direction over both the LT and Southend lines, to join the Tilbury lines which passed through the station on the south side. Local passenger trains from the St Pancras line were provided with a branch from the main flyover, taking them down to a platform on the north side of the station. A second flyover carried westbound District line trains, which, to facilitate interchange in the station, were on the south side of the Southend line, across to the north side to re-join the eastbound London Transport track.

When the first photograph was taken, the arrangement of tracks had not changed greatly. The lines from the Forest Gate direction were on the north side, with the combined lines for Tilbury and Southend on the south and the LT electrified tracks in the centre. However, new tracks were in position on the extreme south side, with a new signal not yet in use. In the space between the new tracks and the up and down lines for Tilbury and Southend, work had commenced on one wall of the flyover. On the north side, beyond all the tracks, work on

the branch of the flyover was well advanced. The signal gantry and posts appear to be contemporary with the 1908 re-arrangement at Barking, to receive the Metropolitan District trains. The arms, both upper and lower quadrant, are of later date. Already the connections from the down line to the LT tracks and to the northern tracks in Barking Station were out of use, and the signal arms controlling access to them had been removed from the posts on the gantry. The Barking West down outer home signal was pulled off for a freight train, and the splitting distant arms show that it was bound for the line to Tilbury. The up signals were also off, indicating the imminence of an up train. The freight train, with its loose-coupled collection of miscellaneous rolling stock hauled by an LMS Fowler Mogul running tender first, was presumably a local working.

The next view, taken approximately 6 months later, shows a second wall in position and work on both the main flyover and its branch well advanced. The original up track has been removed, and trains are using the new track shown in the previous view. The signal gantry has been scrapped and plain steel posts with upper quadrant arms control the up and down tracks. The down train of LMS compartment stock is hauled by BR Standard 2-6-4T No.80100. This was built at Brighton Works in 1955 and withdrawn in 1965. As was usual on the LTS Railway, the locomotive was running bunker first in the down direction.

When the third photograph was taken, work on the main flyover had made further progress, and the branch to the north side of the station was already in use. Construction had started, in between the other two works, on the flyover for westbound LT trains. At this stage both up and down Tilbury and Southend trains were running to the south of the new flyover, and in the photograph an up train of LMS compartment stock is passing. A westbound LT train is also in view; the eastbound track is visible just below the branch flyover. This carries a train from the St Pancras line, also of LMS compartment stock and hauled by an LMS 4F 0-6-0 freight locomotive.

The fourth view shows the completed work. The main flyover runs across the centre of the picture. That carrying the westbound District line obscures the branch flyover to be seen in the previous three views. Overhead live wires have been provided on all LTS tracks, including the flyover, which is used by electric trains to reach a depot. Set 243, built at York and Doncaster in 1959, forms an up train from the Tilbury line to Fenchurch Street. A colour light signal has replaced the semaphore shown in the 1958 view. The changes at Barking belong to that time in the late fifties when expensive schemes to improve track capacity and train services were in full spate on British Railways.

As mentioned above, the LTSR went through a phase of rapid development in the 1880s. In 1884, their line was extended to Shoeburyness. Southend changed from a terminal to a station both with through platforms and terminal bays. In 1889 the GE opened their rival route with its terminal at Southend Victoria, and the LTS responded with further improvements to their Southend Station. However, although from a traffic point of view it was one of the main LTS stations, it never approached the grandeur of Brighton, with its magnificent overall roofs. The three views selected show Southend in steam days.

The first was taken from the overbridge at the west or London end of the station on a busy day in August. While its basic services terminated in London at Fenchurch Street, Southend has always received excursions from a variety of places, the one in the foreground having come from the LNW via the North London line. The main line stock is being propelled by the train engine into a terminal bay, ready for the return journey. The locomotive is Fowler 2-6-0 No.42870 built at Crewe in 1930 and withdrawn in 1963. It carries the train reporting number on the smoke box door. Another excursion, probably from the Midland line, waits in the siding on the left, headed by a 4F 0-6-0. At this time the signalling was still traditional, with LMS type upper quadrant arms controlling departures from 5 of the 6 platforms. The points were manually operated, and such features as point rodding, a trap for the siding, and a crossover with a double slip appear in the photograph. The platforms were numbered 1 to 6, the through platforms being 2 and 3; the return excursion is backing into No.5. The amount of coupling and uncoupling required probably accounts for the shunters hut, but the white paint on the wall behind it is less explicable. Facilities were provided for the watering and coaling of locomotives. One of the water cranes is visible to the right of the signal box, and the coaling platform appears on the right of the photograph. The signal box was demolished in 1961.

The other two photographs were both taken from the London end of platform 2 with about 50 years between them. Neither show very much of the station, but features of interest include the wooden platform and the lengthy canopies. The earlier view shows the locomotive in LTS green livery and the coaches in varnished teak, little different from the livery adopted by the LNER. Coaches of this type, with bogies and electric light, were placed in service from 1903. As the LTS had so short a main line, compartments were the rule, with no catering facilities and very few lavatories. Again, because of the short distances, all the LTS locomotives except two were tank engines, with the 4-4-2 wheel arrangement very much the favourite. No.44 'Prittlewell' was built by Dubs in 1898. It later became LMS No.2142, then BR No.41960, and was withdrawn in 1951. Features of the Tilbury line included the LTSR plate on the top lamp bracket for the information of GE signalmen between Gas Factory Junction and Fenchurch Street, the Westinghouse air brake pump and the two jacks for re-railing carried in front of the smokebox. The destination of trains was indicated by a board carried on the buffer beam or the bunker, according to direction. As all the locomotives were named after places on or near the LTS and associated lines, it is hoped that intending passengers observed the board, and not the name painted on the side tank. Other features are the side chains provided in addition to the screw coupling and the outside cylinders, which were an almost universal feature on Tilbury locomotives. The ends of Midland railway gas-lit coaches are visible in platforms 4 and 5.

The third view was taken in 1959, and shows a Fenchurch Street train running into platform 3 on a summer evening. The first two coaches are of LNE design and reflect the transfer of the LTS from the London Midland to the Eastern Region in 1949. The remainder are standard LMS compartment coaches. Locomotive No.42512 belonged to a series of 37 locomotives built specially for the Tilbury section at Derby in 1934, and was withdrawn in 1960. They were standard 2-6-4 tank locomotives, except for the provision of three cylinders in place of two in order to reduce hammer-blow on the LNE's viaduct between Gas Factory Junction and Fenchurch Street. The practice of carrying destination boards on steam locomotives was not revived after the war. It has however returned with the roller blind indicators of electric multiple unit stock. Apart from the LNER coaches, and the lack of a destination board, this view could have been taken at any time between about 1935 and 1960.

121, 122 Level crossing at Purfleet, on the LTSR (TQ 554782), on 23 May 1959 and 20 January 1977

Purfleet was one of the stations opened on the line to Tilbury in 1854. It was located near a level crossing with the main road, with the platforms projecting into a chalk pit. The original buildings were destroyed by fire in 1902. When the line was electrified in 1961, a new booking office and waiting room was provided on the up side. The goods yard was closed in 1964.

Both the photographs were taken from the footbridge which adjoins the level crossing, looking towards Tilbury. In 1959 the level crossing was protected by conventional gates operated from the adjacent signal box. Their visibility was enhanced with white paint, and painting was in progress in May 1959. There was a red target in the centre, and red lights showed at night. The signalman may be seen with his hand resting on the wheel which operated the gates; needless to say, they were provided with locks suitably linked to the semaphore signals. The signal box was of a standard Midland Railway design, with such characteristic features as a hipped roof, sliding windows, and an external gallery for window cleaning. In addition to operating the gates and functioning as a block post on the main line, Purfleet signal box controlled access to the exchange sidings serving Corys Wharf and the

Thames Board Mills. The cranes, with grabs for discharging coal, are visible on the right of the photograph, and a privately-owned diesel locomotive is partly obscured by the signal box. The Thames Board Mills appear on the left of the photograph and Littlebrook Power Station may be seen on the opposite side of the River Thames. The seven-coach up train consists of 5 LMS compartment coaches and 2 of BR design. The locomotive BR 2-6-4T No.80136 was built at Brighton Works in 1956 and withdrawn in 1965, after an incredibly short life of 9 years.

The photograph of 1977 shows the line after overhead electrification, but the container train from Tilbury Docks is diesel hauled by Class 47/4 No.47423, formerly No.D1534, built by Brush in 1963. The crossing gates have been replaced by lifting barriers, protected by warning lights and operated from the signal box. Externally this is virtually unchanged, although the Midland style nameboard, with white lettering on black, has been replaced by a BR version with black lettering on white. The Thames Board Mills and Corys continue to generate traffic, although with the latter the emphasis has changed from coal to oil. The two photographs however, provide a contrast in trains and level crossings.

123, 124 Upminster, formerly LTSR (TQ 562868), on 22 August 1926 and 24 March 1956

The LTSR cut-off line between Barking and Pitsea was opened as far as Upminster in 1885. At the time, the GER were considering branches to both Southend and Tilbury. The GE branch to Southend was opened in 1889, but the route to Tilbury was blocked by the LTSR, who opened their own line from Romford to West Thurrock Junction near Grays on the Tilbury line. The line was opened in two sections, that from the east end of Upminster Station to West Thurrock Junction being completed in 1892, and the line from west of Upminster to Romford in 1893. Upminster's position as a junction was reflected in the provision of a reversible loop line on the down side, serving the back of the down platform. After the Whitechapel and Bow Railway was opened in 1902, a few District steam trains were extended to Upminster, but these workings ended in 1905 when the District was electrified. However, revival came in 1932 when the line from Barking to Upminster was quadrupled, with two electrified tracks for District trains on the down side. Upminster Station was rebuilt and became the outer terminal for electric trains, with a significant effect on the rate of growth of its commuter traffic.

The first view was taken from the up platform before rebuilding. The train, bearing its Southend destination board, consists of LTS stock. The leading brake van is a four wheeler, and the remainder of the train appears to consist of either 4 or 6 wheel compartment stock. This was not the best that could be offered in 1926, but is the type of stock that would be in use on busy weekends in August. The locomotive is still in Midland red livery, and bears its Midland number on the smokebox door. No.58 of the LTS 51 class was built by Sharp Stewart in 1900. It was originally named 'Hornsey Road', became 'Hornsey' in 1911, and lost its name and changed its number to 2165 after the Midland take over in 1912. It later became LMS No.2099 and was withdrawn in 1951. In 1926 some of the LTS features, such as the Westinghouse brake, were still in use, but the jacks had been removed from their prominent position at the front end. In the down direction

it was more usual to be running bunker first, but if a locomotive had worked via the terminus at Tilbury and had not been on a turntable, then it would run smokebox first, as shown in this view. The signal box, with its gable end and bargeboards, is typical of the LTS, but the bracket signal is of Midland design. The left-hand arm applies to the up main line and the right-hand to the Romford branch.

The second view was taken from the footbridge at the eastern end of the station in 1956, 24 years after the rebuilding. The original LTS buildings of 1885 are visible on the extreme left, but from 1932 the main entrance was from the road bridge. Three platforms were provided, that on the south side having a bay used mainly by trains from Grays, and the other two being island platforms. In 1956 the main up and down platforms were numbered 1 and 2, and those used by the LT electric trains were 3, 4, and 5. The tracks for 1 and 2 were not electrified and therefore not accessible to LT trains, but all platforms could be used by BR trains if required. The photograph shows an LT train on the left ready to leave for Richmond, Surrey in platform 3. All the cars towards the rear end of the train are of the clerestory roof type constructed between 1923 and 1931. In 1956 District line trains still carried oil lamps at the rear. A three-coach push-pull train has arrived on the right at platform 4 from Romford. After the electrification of the Shenfield line, LNER N7 class tank locomotives were readily available, and provided a replacement for the Midland 0-4-4 tank locomotives which had been fitted with push-pull equipment for working the services between Romford, Grays and Tilbury. No.69695 was built by Beardmore in 1927. It was fitted with push-pull gear in 1951 for working from Annesley near Nottingham, was transferred to the LTS in 1955 and withdrawn in 1958. The two photographs were taken during the first and second phases of the development of Upminster; a third phase began with the electrification of the LTS lines in 1961.

125, 126 North Walsham Town Station, formerly Midland & Great Northern Joint Committee, (TG 232298), on 17 August 1958 and 29 June 1968

North Walsham, a modest Norfolk market town, had two stations until 1959, not on account of its traffic potential but rather because it was served by two railways. The East Norfolk Railway reached it from the Norwich direction in 1874 and was extended to Cromer in 1877. The Yarmouth and North Norfolk Railway approached from Yarmouth, reaching North Walsham in 1881. Instead of joining the East Norfolk, which formed part of the GE system, a link to Melton Constable in 1883 connected it to the Eastern and Midlands Railway. In 1893 the Eastern and Midlands was taken over jointly and, until nationalisation in 1948, operated as the Midland and Great Northern Joint Railway.

The first view shows the Midland and Great Northern station after absorption by British Railways. The M&GN was basically a single track railway, but North Walsham was a passing place. Trains were controlled from a Midland-style signal box with conventional manually-operated points and signals. The train approaching was a Birmingham to Yarmouth train of LMS coaches hauled by LMS type 2-6-0 No.43158. This was built at Doncaster Works in 1952 and withdrawn in 1965. Seven passengers are waiting to join the train; there seems to be a porter waiting by the exit, perhaps for ticket collecting. By East Anglian standards, the station was simple. The main buildings were on the eastbound platform, built to an H-

plan, with the gables of the outer ends ornamented with boards to give an impression of timber framing. There was a waiting room on the westbound platform, and both buildings had canopies supported by brackets. Three features were noteworthy. First, the footbridge was reached by conventional wooden steps, but the span across the tracks consisted of a trussed girder. Second the fence with its crossed palings, was characteristic of the M&GN. Third, the six fire buckets were arranged at two levels outside the gentlemen's lavatory. Other features, such as the gas lamps were conventional. The only signal in view was the westbound starter, an upper quadrant just visible over the top of the locomotive.

The second view, taken about 9 years after closure, shows the extent of demolition and the onslaught of nature. The footbridge and the signal box have gone, the site of the latter being indicated by the hole in the platform wall, formerly occupied by rods and wires. Metal objects are particularly appropriate for removal, including lamp posts. Grass has begun to take root on the platforms and young trees are growing on the track bed. The speed at which stations disappear depends on a number of factors, including the possibility of alternative use for the site. At North Walsham it would seem that after 9 years nobody has yet purchased the site for other uses.

127, 128 St Albans Abbey Station, formerly LNWR (TL 144063), on 28 September 1946 and 31 March 1973

St Albans, a cathedral city of moderate size, was served by three railway companies. It was reached by a branch from the LNW at Watford in 1858, and from the GN at Hatfield in 1865. The GN opened its own station, but its trains ran through to the LNW terminal to provide interchange facilities. The Midland's extension to London ran through St Albans, and their station was opened in 1867. The GN service was withdrawn in 1951 and their through station was closed to passengers. Abbey Station, however, continues to be served from Watford Junction.

The first view shows the station in virtually its original form. The most striking feature is the overall roof with its beams and pillars resembling those to be seen at Euston. This fulfilled the dual purpose of protecting waiting passengers, and rolling stock – which could be left for the night. It extended beyond the buildings, but did not cover the bay platform used by GN. The buildings had a strong LNW flavour, conveyed by such details as the chimneys and the gable ends. The goods yard is visible on the right and, beyond it, a gasholder forming part of the gasworks. The push-pull train from Watford occupies the main platform, with an LNE train from Hatfield in the bay. The locomotive is Fowler 2-6-2 tank No.10, built at Derby

Works in 1930 and withdrawn in 1961. In addition to its number, the smokebox door carries the shed plate IC, indicating that No.10 was allocated to Watford Shed.

Considerable changes came in the 1950s with the withdrawal of the Hatfield service, the substitution of experimental railcars for the push-pull steam train, and modifications to the overall roof. However, by the time the second photograph was taken, in 1973, even greater changes had taken place. The station buildings and overall roof have been demolished, the only accommodation consisting of a very simple shelter, the graffiti reflecting the absence of railway staff. Electric lighting has replaced gas, and the few signs that are provided, such as the name of the station, have standard BR lettering. The tracks have been removed from the goods yard and the bay, only a single platform line being retained. All the signals and the signal cabin have been removed. The gas works has closed. The photograph shows the rail car approaching from Watford and typifies the minimal facilities imposed by the economic conditions of the 1970s. The only thing left from the old station is a platform surface formed of flagstones.

129, 130 Southend Pier Railway, (TQ 884850), in 1872 and on 25 April 1970

When the rapid development of Southend as a seaside resort had commenced, its communication with London by steamer became increasingly important. A pier was opened in 1830, and by 1846 this had reached a length of $1\frac{1}{4}$ miles, so that steamers could come alongside at all states of the tide. A single line railway with wooden rails was provided, motive power being men, or a sail when the wind was suitable. This was replaced in 1875 with iron rails and horse traction. After six years, the horses had imposed considerable wear on the decking, the rails had spread and closure became necessary. People had to make their own way along the pier until a new single track electric railway was opened in 1890. Its capacity was increased by the provision of passing loops up until 1930, when the track was doubled with two scissors crossovers controlled by signal boxes, each about 200 yards from the terminal stations. This arrangement continued until 1970; then, as an economy measure, the crossovers, signalling and signal boxes were removed, the amount of rolling stock in service was reduced, and the railway became two parallel single lines.

The first view is a copy of a photograph with the caption 'Pier Trams, Southend, 1872'. It shows iron flat-bottomed rails spiked directly to the decking of the bridge. The train is made up of 3 4-wheel coaches, with a small trolley at the front for the driver. The motive power consists of two horses in tandem. There is no visible facility for moving the driver's trolley to the opposite end of the train for a return journey, so either there was a corresponding trolley on the other end, or else the trolley was moved over the decking of the pier. The pier was commanded by a master mariner, and this is reflected in the nautical uniforms of the staff which, in addition to the driver, seems to include a petty officer and two able seamen. Also to be seen are the iron railings and the shoreward end buildings. As the rails seemed to bear directly on the deck, with no re-inforcement in the form of a horse track or sleepers,

it is perhaps not surprising that after six years the railway was unusable. It will be noted that the date on the photograph conflicts with documentary evidence, which indicates an opening date of 1875.

The second view shows the Pier Railway at what was probably its maximum development. This was reached in 1930, as far as track was concerned, with doubling, with scissors crossings and with signal cabins adjacent to the line at each end. The 1970 view was taken from the signal cabin at the shore end of the pier. It shows the flat bottom rails spiked to longitudinal sleepers at 3 ft 6 in gauge with a third rail, carrying 550v d.c., located between the running rails. The scissors crossover was manually-operated, with facing point locking bars, and electrical detection. Colour light signals were provided, and when the signal boxes were manned normal double line working operated between the two crossovers. However, during periods with light traffic the signal cabins could be switched out and the railway could be worked as a single line, using either of the tracks. This was the case when the photograph was taken. One of the 4 seven-coach trains delivered in 1949 is passing in the direction of the shore. These were constructed by A.C. Cars Ltd of Thames Ditton, and consisted of 3 motors and 4 trailers, with motors at each end and in the middle of the trains. Features include air-operated doors and an ample provision of windows to afford sea views. As mentioned above, the crossovers and signalling have now been removed, and the railway is operated as two separate single lines, each with its own train. Two seven-coach trains are retained, 5 coaches are kept for replacements, and the remainder were dismantled. Initially, the train on the west line consisted of coach Nos. 22, 23, 24, 25, 17, 27 and 28, of which No. 22 appears on the end in the photograph. The survival of the railway depends upon the survival of Southend Pier.

5 The West of England

The broad gauge Bristol and Exeter Railway was opened as far as Bridgewater in 1841, and finally reached Exeter in 1844. Highbridge was one of the original stations. The Somerset Central (also a broad gauge line) linked Highbridge Wharf to Glastonbury from 1854, replacing the Glastonbury Canal. It crossed the B&E on the level just north of Highbridge Station. This arrangement was not opposed by the B&E, who operated the Somerset Central as part of the broad gauge empire. Absorption of the Somerset Central by the B&E might have been anticipated, but instead the small company conceived an ambition to form part of a land link between South Wales and France, and to transfer to the standard gauge system. In 1858 an extension from Highbridge Wharf to a passenger pier at Burnham was opened, and by 1862 rail communication was complete between Burnham and Wimborne, on the LSWR line to Poole. The Somerset Central joined the Dorset Central, to form the Somerset and Dorset Railway, and the level crossing at Highbridge became far more important. Financial difficulties might yet have landed the S&D in the Great Western camp, but after some intricate

negotiations an Act of 1876 confirmed its leasing to the Midland and London & South Western companies. (The S&D Bath Extension had connected it with the Midland.) It retained a degree of independence until 1930, when the Southern assumed responsibility for track and signalling, and the LMS for locomotives and most of the rolling stock. After the advent of British Rail, the western section passed into the hands of the Western Region, who were then in a position to do something about the Highbridge level crossing. The passenger service between Highbridge and Burnham was withdrawn in 1951, but the line remained open until 1963. The S&D Highbridge Station, with its three terminal and one through platform road was closed to passengers, along with most of the S&D, in 1966.

The first view was taken from the London end of the Great Western down platform, which in BR days became platform 6. The Great Western signal box on the right, in addition to acting as a block post on the main line, controlled the level crossing. The up starter is of typical GW design, with wooden post and metal finial, located in a restricted space. This is the reason for the placing of the

pivot of the lower quadrant arm in the centre, and the incorporation of one of the spectacles in the arm, instead of in a separate spectacle plate. The trackwork includes three crossings. All that appears of the station is the end of the canopy on the up platform and the ramps at the end of each platform, with notices warning passengers against crossing the line. Whereas the S&D continued to use a level-crossing, road traffic was diverted to the steel girder bridge which crosses the picture. The train is pulled by locomotive No.1370, a Johnson 0-4-4T built by the Midland Railway. It was allocated BR No.58067 and was withdrawn in 1953. The compartment coach was built for the S&DR.

By 1962, although the regular passenger service to Burnham had not run for eleven years, there had been no major changes in the layout. The view is from the GW up platform, numbered 7 by BR. The centre balance signal arm remains the same, but minor changes include the addition of cowls to protect the underside of the bridge from the exhaust of steam locomotives and the substitution of a reworded (but still GWR) warning notice at the end of the platform. A stop sign for 6 car diesel trains is an obvious addition, but the platform trolleys are of traditional style. A multiple unit diesel penetrates the right side

of the photograph.

The third view of the Highbridge crossing was taken from platform 5 of the S&D station. (Although there were only three terminal tracks and one through line in the S&D station, one of the tracks had a platform on both sides, so there were 5 platform faces.) It was taken on a wet and cold winter's day, when the S&D was traversed by the LCGB Special Train, the 'Mendip Merchantman'. The train ran over the level-crossing into the GW up sidings, and then backed into the GW down platform. The photograph shows (partly obscured) BR 2-10-0 No.92243, at the head of the train, facing in the up direction but standing at the down platform. This locomotive was built at Crewe Works in 1958 and withdrawn in 1965. The GW signal box is visible above the steps and the S&D box, closed in 1914, appears on the right of the track leading to the level crossing. Just showing on the extreme left is a notice indicating that a climb onto the bridge is necessary for passengers wishing to reach platforms 1, 2, 3, 4, or 7. By this time the S&D Highbridge Works had been abandoned by the railway for 36 years, and only 6 years passed before the final demise of the S&D at Highbridge.

134, 135 Norton Fitzwarren Junction, formerly GWR (ST 194255), on 7 June 1921 and 17 August 1973

The broad gauge Bristol and Exeter was opened in stages, reaching Beambridge near Wellington in 1843, and Exeter in 1844. The branch to Minehead reached Watchet in 1862 and its terminus in 1874. The second branch to leave the main line at Norton Fitzwarren originally had its physical junction with the Minehead branch and not direct with the main line. This was the Barnstaple branch, completed in 1873. Major changes took place in the 1930s. In particular, at the end of 1931, new island platforms were brought into use, and early in 1932 quadruple track was provided to a point beyond the junction, together with a new signal box. In 1937 the Barnstaple line was altered to join the main line instead of the Minehead branch. Norton Fitzwarren Station was closed to passengers in 1961. With the decline of holiday traffic, the Barnstaple line was closed to passengers in 1960. The four track section was cut back to Silk Mill Crossing, just over a mile west of Taunton, in 1970, although the up relief line was retained as part of a single line to Minehead until it was taken out of use in the January of 1971.

The two views show Norton Fitzwarren Junction before the developments of the 1930s and after the decline in the 1960s. The first view was taken from the footbridge at the west end of the old station. The main line displays the wide spacing of tracks found on former broad gauge railways. The Minehead branch swings round to the right, with the Barnstaple line forking off it to run some distance parallel with the main line. To the right of the signal cabin, pick-up apparatus for the collection of tokens for the two single

line branches is visible. The signal arms are of the same type as that shown in photos 131 and 132, pivoted centrally with a spectacle incorporated. As might be expected because of masking by the footbridge, there are two arms for the main line, the upper of which projects above the level of the footbridge. But the signals for the Barnstaple and Minehead lines have only single arms which would not be visible from any distance. Presumably, as all trains would have either stopped at the station or at least slowed to collect the token, this was not considered a danger.

The second view was taken from the bridge connecting the two new island platforms; the site of the old footbridge was roughly in line with the fixed distant signal on the Minehead line. Some vestiges of the elaborate layout of the 1930s remain, mainly in the form of ballast without tracks. However, the point at which the former up relief track joined the Minehead line is fairly clear in the right foreground. Somewhat surprisingly, the most striking survival is the overground telegraph wires. The tracks, laid with continuous welded rail, were placed closer together to save space when the line was quadrupled. The Barnstaple line has gone, but one track of the Minehead line survives, together with a section of the up relief to give a connection to Taunton. This is out of use, but the enthusiasts responsible for the re-opening of part of the branch hope to revive the service to Taunton. The up express is being hauled by a diesel-hydraulic locomotive of the Western class. Above all, this view shows the decline in the quantity of railways.

Exeter St David's was an important crossroads between the Great Western and the LSW routes to the West. From the north the Bristol and Exeter arrived in 1844. To the south, the South Devon reached Newton Abbot in 1846 and Plymouth in 1848. The LSW route from Waterloo was opened to Exeter in 1860. When it was completed in 1851 the Exeter and Crediton was part of the broad gauge empire, but with appropriate machinations it became the first step in the LSW advance to Cornwall. Through St David's GW down trains were heading south, but LSW down trains were pointing north. This complication was less significant than the fact that all LSW trains had to cross the GW main lines. Since the advent of BR and the transfer of lines to the Western Region, the number of trains executing this manoeuvre has been much reduced. All the trains from Waterloo are terminated at St David's, but the very few running between Exmouth and Barnstaple still make the crossing. The two views show one up freight train serving the former LSW lines and one down express.

The freight train consists of an interesting collection of loose coupled open wagons and vans, hauled by a former LSW 700 class locomotive No.30691. This was built by Dubs in 1897 and withdrawn in 1961. For the climb at 1 in 37 between St David's and Exeter Central, a pilot locomotive has been provided. This is BR 2-6-2T No.82013 built at Swindon Works in 1952 and withdrawn in 1964. In the days of steam, additional engines were usually provided for the climb, thus increasing operating problems at St David's. The train is running through the centre road between platforms 1 and 3. The building of 1864 is visible on the right, but the rest of the station belongs mainly to the period 1911 to 1914, with subsequent modifications. The signal gantry supports the signals for all three tracks; the lower quadrant for Central is obscured by the exhaust of the pilot locomotive. The centre balance arm on the left has its counterweight above the gantry. Cowls are provided to diminish the corrosive effects of the smoke from steam locomotives. As this view shows, locomotives started the climb with a very full head of steam.

The second view, like the first, was taken from the end of

platform 3, looking north. Although going in the same direction as the up freight, the train shown is a down express calling at St David's. The coaches are BR Mk1 in maroon livery, except for the second coach, which is painted in GW chocolate and cream. The locomotive is Warship class No.D800, built at Swindon Works in 1958 and withdrawn in 1968. All the signals are on, and the train is stationary – for many years, at least by Southern standards, GW station stops tended to protraction. The speed restriction sign of 25 mph applies to the curve at the end of the platform onto the down main line. It is not difficult to appreciate the attraction of the railway scene at this point, and evidently it was appreciated by the two Boy Scouts who appear in both photographs.

138, 139, 140 Main line at Dawlish, formerly GWR (SX 963765), in the 1880s, in 1902 and on 10 February 1977

As mentioned above, the South Devon Railway was opened between Exeter and Newton Abbot in 1846. This section was originally designed for atmospheric traction, but there is no evidence of this in any of the photographs. The track was converted to standard gauge in 1892, without passing through an intermediate stage with mixed gauge. In 1902 widening of the sea wall was completed, followed in October 1905 by the doubling of the track. Between the wars plans were made for relocating the main line inland in a less exposed position, but these failed to materialise.

The first view shows the front at Dawlish perhaps 40 years after the construction of the sea wall, carrying the railway which separated town and beach. Conventional broad gauge track is shown with bridge rail laid on longitudinal sleepers with wooden transoms holding them in position. The original portal of Kennaway Tunnel is shown and to the right of it a crossbar signal. (Few of these survived on the main line after 1890.) The vegetation suggests a summer view, but somewhat surprisingly there is not a soul in sight.

The second view was taken looking in the opposite direction, between June 1902, when locomotive No.100 was named, and not later than November 1902, when it appeared in the *Locomotive Magazine*. The most probable date would be during the summer of 1902. At this time

the name carried was 'Dean', marking the retirement of William Dean, Locomotive and Carriage Superintendent of the GWR 1877 until 1902. Although in its essential features No.100 was the first of the 'Saint' class, it had some distinctive features, particularly the framing. Various changes took place, including re-boilering and re-numbering before withdrawal in 1932. No.100 displays many of the characteristic features of the products of Swindon, including the copper-rimmed chimney and brass safety valve cover. The train, described on the photograph as a Plymouth express, has a variety of coaching stock. Clerestory roofs are in evidence; most coaches built after 1904 had rounded roofs. This view belongs to a period of rapid development on the Great Western.

The third view was taken from the same footbridge as the 1902 view, but about 75 years later. Whereas the first view showed broad gauge track and the second bullhead rail held in chairs secured to wooden sleepers, the third shows continuous welded rail on concrete sleepers. In the foreground a finial, part of a semaphore arm and the top of a sighting board are visible. The train is a Paignton express consisting of BR Mk2 coaches hauled by a Class 50 diesel electric locomotive No.50035. The background shows a few changes in the Victorian housing which borders the railway, but many of the buildings, including the conspicuous house with the twin turrets, appear in both photographs. On balance, there has been less change in the buildings than in the railway.

141, 142 Chalford Station, formerly GWR (SO 900024), in 1903 and 24 May 1968

The Cheltenham and Great Western Union Railway opened a line from Swindon to Kemble Junction, with a branch to Cirencester, in 1841. The company was taken over by the GWR in 1843, and the line to Standish Junction for Gloucester was completed in 1845. It was converted from broad to standard gauge in 1872. The Stroud valley was well populated and a new station was opened at Chalford in 1897. When the GW were looking for suitable lines on which to cultivate local traffic by means of steam rail motor cars calling at halts, the Stroud Valley section of the Swindon to Gloucester line was the first to be allocated a service. Two cars were put into service between Stonehouse and Chalford in 1903, calling at the existing stations and also at recognised stopping places without platforms. (These were later replaced by halts.) The local service was successful for many years but finally succumbed to road competition in 1964.

Initially Chalford was a conventional wayside station, with a single storey brick building with the usual facilities on the up side, and a shelter on the down side. However, seven years later when the rail motor service was introduced in the Stroud valley it became, in effect, a local terminus. As the first view shows, it already had a signal box, and sidings and a small engine shed were provided beyond the box on the up side. The combination of additional stopping places and increased services brought an eightfold increase in passenger traffic in the Stroud valley, and by 1908 the GW had 100 steam rail motor cars in use in various parts of their system. It has not proved possible to identify the car shown in the photograph. It has arrived from Stonehouse and is apparently running forward, either into the siding or back over the crossover onto the down line. Other items of interest include the gas lamps, the loading gauge in the goods

siding, and the advertisement for Roger's Ales of Chalford on the down side waiting room.

Chalford was closed to passengers in 1964. The first sign of decline was the removal of the engine shed in about 1935, but facilities for one locomotive to be stabled in the open were retained until 1951. The goods sidings, shown in the first view to the left of the station, were closed in 1963 and removed in 1964; the signal box and remaining sidings and crossover were taken out of use in 1965. The second view shows the scene in 1968, by which time the buildings and both platforms had been demolished. A useful fix is given by Milepost 98, visible on the up side; the station was 98 miles 1 chain from Paddington. Some buildings in use by permanent way staff may be seen beyond the site of the signal box. There are some new concrete bins for track ballast. However, the most significant feature is the empty ground, once occupied by a passenger station and its goods sidings.

143, 144 Christow Station, formerly GWR (SX 839865), about 1903 and on 10 February 1977

The broad gauge Moretonhampstead and South Devon Railway was opened from the South Devon main line at Newton Abbot to Moretonhampstead in 1866. After several abortive attempts, the Teign Valley Railway Company opened its standard gauge line from Heathfield on the Moretonhampstead line to Christow in 1882. Originally the village of Christow was served by Ashton Station, and the terminal of the branch handled goods traffic only. In 1892 the Moretonhampstead line was converted to standard gauge and the isolation of the Teign Valley Railway ended. In 1903 the Exeter Railway Company opened its line from Exeter to an end-on junction with the Teign Valley at Christow. A new station was built with passenger facilities, a passing loop and signals. Taken together, the Exeter Railway, the Teign Valley and the Moretonhampstead and South Devon provided an alternative route to the main line between Exeter and Newton Abbot. With this in mind, the length of the passing loop at Christow was extended in 1943. The run-down of the line began with the withdrawal of the passenger service in 1958. Complete closure came in stages, between Christow and the outskirts of Exeter in 1958, in the opposite direction from Christow to Trusham in 1961, and then in sections until closure to the junction at Heathfield in 1968.

The first view was taken from the overbridge at the south end of Christow Station, on a summer morning not long after the opening of the line through to Exeter. Clearly the train was stopped long enough for everybody to look at the camera. In addition to the driver and fireman of the locomotive, there are five railwaymen on the

platform. The solitary figure on the up platform or the two people on the down might have been passengers. The train consisted of three compartment coaches, one of which carried a clerestory roof. Backless cabs of the type shown on the locomotive were still to be found on the LMS and GW railways after the Second World War. The station buildings consist of a single-storey brick edifice on the up side and a waiting room on the down. The diagonally placed palings in the fence, with their suggestion of the Midland Railway rather than the GW, were presumably the work of the independent company who built the station. The white painted lamp posts, still looking new and spruce, supported oil lamps. New paint is also in evidence on the gate leading into the station yard and on the gate of the occupation crossing near the end of the passing loop. In contrast, the signal cabin looks a little drab. A siding to some stone quarries left from the back of the goods yard, but this is not visible.

It is unlikely that any of the station staff eyeing the camera in 1903 would have anticipated that 74 years later a lawn would be growing where the train was standing. The second view shows the way the buildings and platforms have been adapted to form a residence. Alterations include the new roof on the main building, with gable ends instead of hips, and some doors replaced by windows. The chimneys have also been altered, but the waiting room on the down side shows little external change. Perhaps the most striking survivals are the platforms and the length of fencing, with its diagonal paling. Even with necessary alterations, the original function of the buildings remains clear.

145, 146 Bovey Tracey Station, formerly GWR (SX 811782), about 1900 and on 12 March 1965

As mentioned above, the broad gauge Moretonhampstead and South Devon Railway was opened in 1866 and Bovey Tracey was one of the original stations. Conversion to standard gauge was carried out in 1892. The passenger service was withdrawn in 1959, and subsequently the branch has been cut back, to Bovey in 1964 and to Heathfield in 1970.

Both views were taken from the level crossing at the south end of the station. The first was taken during the period after 1892 when the gauge had been narrowed by sawing off the ends of the transoms and moving one line of longitudinal sleepers and bridge rails towards the other. It shows the reason for the wide gap between the rails which is still a feature of many Great Western stations. At this time Bovey had all the features of a branch line station serving a small town. It was provided with a goods shed, visible beyond the platform awning, and at the side of the goods yard, on the right of the photograph, there was a warehouse. The signal cabin projects beyond the goods

shed, and the passing loop was fully signalled with the standard GW signals of the day. Signal wires and point rodding border the left hand side of the track. The telegraph line is also on the left. Fencing consists of wooden posts and wire.

By the time the second view was taken the passenger service had been withdrawn and Bovey had become the terminus of the line, but this had not led to major changes. In fact the most striking change, the substitution of bullhead rail and transverse sleepers for bridge rail, had nothing to do with the downgrading of the branch. However, the signal box was closed when the passenger service was withdrawn in 1959, and subsequently the box and the signals were removed. But features such as the station building with its canopy, the goods shed and the warehouse all remain. Even the telegraph line and the fencing show no change. However, visits by a passenger diesel train from Newton Abbot marked the final closure in 1970, and abandonment has now left its mark.

147, 148 Newquay Harbour, (SW 808620), about 1900 and on 9 August 1964

By the beginning of the nineteenth century Cornwall was experiencing rapid economic growth, based on its production of clay and mineral ores. Most of the production went away by sea, and in 1836 a harbour was opened at Newquay. In 1849 this was linked to nearby producing districts by the horse worked railway of J.T. Treffry. It reached the harbour by a rope-worked incline which descended through a tunnel at 1 in $4\frac{1}{2}$. The line was upgraded and connected to a line from Fowey in 1874, to form part of the Cornish Minerals Railway system. Passenger services to a station in the town began in 1876, and in 1877 the GWR took over operations. Newquay became more of a resort and less of a port, so passenger traffic increased and freight to the harbour declined. Clay exports were concentrated on the more accessible ports of the south coast, including Par and Fowey. Coal and clay traffic ceased in 1921, and when the fish traffic ended in 1926 the line down to the harbour was closed.

The first view shows the harbour with railway tracks in position, but not much evidence of traffic. There are two ketch-rigged cargo vessels in the harbour, one alongside the quay and one laying off. A single wagon, which seems to have the whiteness associated with china clay, is on the outer quay. Of particular interest is the island quay, connected by a wooden viaduct. Apart from the two cargo vessels, the harbour is in use by small fishing boats, and at the time of the photograph was evidently not very busy, although the construction of the island quay suggests greater traffic in times past.

The second view shows the harbour with no freight traffic and no rail connection. The tunnel, which once carried the railway track to busy quays, has had its lower section adapted to house an aquarium. The quays, instead of carrying clay and mineral ores, are thronged by the parked cars of summer visitors. The viaduct has been removed from the island quay, which only serves as a mooring post. There are no freight vessels, but there are a fair number of small fishing vessels and pleasure craft. The two photographs show the way in which a harbour has changed its function and character, and has lost its railway.

PORTLAND HARBOUR FROM OLD HILL

149 Merchant's Railway at Portland, (SY 689738), about 1930

The Merchant's Railway had some points in common with Treffry's line down to Newquay Harbour. In both cases a horse-worked line extended inland, with an inclined plane running down to complete the link with water transport. There were, however, some important differences. Opening dates were 1849 for Treffry's line and 1826 for the railway on Portland, the corresponding closure dates being 1926 and 1939. Whereas Treffry's incline was designed to carry a variety of two-way traffic, the Portland Railway was confined to stone travelling downhill. Because of this, plus the fact that it was in a single-line tunnel, the Newquay incline was worked with a stationary engine, while the Portland incline was self-acting. Treffry's line was adapted to form part of the main-line system, but the Merchant's Railway, with its 4 ft 6 in gauge, was never physically connected. However, after the opening of Weymouth and Portland Railway in 1865,

an exchange siding was constructed, so that the stone could be transferred either to ship or standard gauge railway wagon. As mentioned above, the line was closed in 1939, and the track was lifted in 1957. The Portland Railway was a statutory undertaking, known locally not by its official name, but as the Merchant's Railway or Freeman's Incline.

The photograph shows a view at the top of the incline. Motive power is represented by five horses, wearing the harness and chains used for pulling the wagons. As only one traffic was carried only one type of wagon was required, and two examples of the four wheeled trolleys with dumb buffers and no springs are shown. The method of operation was not appreciably changed during the 113 years of operation, and the Merchant's Railway was the outstanding example of a horse worked railway in the West of England.

150, 151, 152 Poole, formerly LSWR (SZ 013910), on 20 September 1958, 20 June 1964 and 11 April 1970

The railway history of the ancient port of Poole is complicated. The port consists mainly of wharves on either side of an inlet from Poole Harbour, the town being located on a spit of land on the east side. The first railway accommodation was provided by a branch from the Southampton and Dorchester Railway, opened in 1847 to a terminus on the west side of the harbour. When the Somerset & Dorset was completed from Burnham to Wimborne, it will be recalled that it regarded itself as a land bridge between South Wales and France, with Burnham and Poole as the trans-shipment points. However, an alternative source of traffic was the growing resort of Bournemouth, and the S&D was behind the Poole and Bournemouth Railway. This linked the S&D and the Southampton and Dorchester at Broadstone to Bournemouth, cutting across the neck of the promontory on which the town of Poole was situated. It reached Poole in 1872, and its terminus at Bournemouth West in 1874.

At this time access to Bournemouth from the London direction was via Christchurch to the terminal at Bournemouth East, so that railways converged on Bournemouth from both east and west. By 1893 a series of new lines and connections were completed, and the old route of the Southampton and Dorchester via Ringwood and Wimborne was short-circuited by the new route via Bournemouth. Poole, in addition to being served by the S&D trains to Bournemouth West, became a station on the main line to Dorchester and Weymouth.

In crossing the neck of the promontory on which Poole was located, the railway cut across the two roads running into the town. The first view shows both level crossings. It was taken from the footbridge adjoining the western of the two, and shows a train leaving for Bournemouth West. This was on the Brockenhurst to Bournemouth West service via Ringwood, Wimborne and Poole. It consists of two LSW coaches, forming Motor Set No.2, propelled by

an M7 class tank locomotive, which is also hauling a van for parcels traffic. The locomotive, No.30107, was constructed at Nine Elms Works in 1905 and withdrawn in 1964. The Brockenhurst to Bournemouth via Ringwood service ended in 1964 when the old route of the Southampton and Dorchester was closed. The check rail indicates the sharpness of the curve, reflecting an alignment diverging sharply from the line which served the east side of the port. It will be noted that the two level crossings effectively cut off Poole, but they were condoned by the Corporation on condition that all trains called at the station. Poole A Signal Cabin is just visible beyond the train. This was a block post, but the small cabin in the right foreground was confined to operating the gates of the Towngate Road crossing. Gates and cabin were taken out of use in 1971, when the new road bridge was opened.

The second photograph was taken from a carriage window on a down express, and shows the bottom of the footbridge from which the first photograph was taken, but looking in the opposite direction. The train consists of a locomotive and coaches, all designed by O.V.S. Bulleid

during his period with the Southern Railway. West Country class locomotive No.34004 was built at Brighton Works in 1945, rebuilt in 1958 and withdrawn in 1967. A small part of the buildings and canopies of the old Poole station can be seen. A standard Southern warning notice adjoins the gates, and an older, non-standard notice forbids improper access to the platform. The up starter is a standard Southern signal, with a two-rail post and an upper quadrant arm.

The third view was taken from a slightly different viewpoint, the up starter signal providing a fix. This shows the electric motor operating the signal. The old station has been demolished, and the new buildings are visible on both up and down sides. To make room for the overbridge which replaced the level crossing the platforms have been relocated. The buildings and lamp posts both reflect the more austere style of British Rail which followed the affluence of the late fifties. The changes at Poole are an example of an opportunity being taken to provide a modern station, largely at the expense of a town improvement scheme.

153, 154, 155 Wareham, formerly LSWR (SY 920882), on 20 June 1964, 29 April 1967 and 10 February 1977

Wareham was one of the original stations on the Southampton and Dorchester Railway. It was opened in 1847 on the east side of the level crossing with the road into the ancient town. In 1885 a branch line was opened from Worgret Junction, 1 mile 7 chains west of Wareham, to the port and seaside resort of Swanage. Most of the branch line services ran from Wareham, and it was decided to open a new station to accommodate the traffic. To avoid the complication of the Swanage trains crossing the road, the new station was opened in 1886 on the west side of the crossing. The passenger service to Swanage was withdrawn at the beginning of 1972, although clay traffic

from Furzebrook Siding was retained. There was no immediate effect on Wareham Station, but subsequently a number of changes have occurred. The crossing keeper's cottages have been demolished, and in May 1976 the tracks in the bay platforms were taken out of use.

The first view was taken shortly after the arrival of the 08.30 express from Waterloo to Weymouth. Passengers are transferring from the Bulleid coaches of the express to the Maunsell-designed stock of the branch train. The locomotive, BR standard 2-6-4 tank No.80146 was built at Brighton works in 1956 and withdrawn in 1967. With the closure of so many branch lines this scene would now

be rare on British railways.

The other two views were both taken from the footbridge adjoining the level crossing at the east end of the station. In the first, the station house of the 1847 station survives, although both platforms have gone. A typical LSW signal box appears on one side of the tracks, and a tall LSW lattice post, with a Southern upper quadrant arm on the other. (In fact the signal box was brought into use by the Southern in 1928.) The up train is hauled by BR standard 2-6-0 No.76005, built at Horwich Works in 1952 and withdrawn in 1967. The more recent view also shows an up train, the 08.38 from Weymouth to Waterloo, leaving Wareham on a very wet and cold winter morning. The train consists of 4-TC Set No.422

propelled by Class 33/1 locomotive No.33103, built by BRCW in 1962. (Electrification begins at Bournemouth, and a 4-REP electric set will provide motive power for the rest of the journey.) Perhaps the most striking change is the demolition of the old station house, revealing the large goods shed. Apart from some painting and the movement of a chimney, the signal box is unchanged; likewise the telegraph poles and signal. Special warning lights, of the type usually used with lifting barriers, have been added to the level crossing gates. A feature of both photographs is the line of oil tankers waiting to be filled with oil from the well at Kimmeridge. Wareham is an example of adaption rather than radical change.

156, 157 Exeter Central Station, formerly LSWR (SY 930919), about 1912 and on 14 April 1971

The LSWR route from Waterloo to Exeter was completed in 1860. Queen Street Station remained a terminus until 1862, when the steeply graded connection to the GW at Exeter St David's was opened as a necessary preliminary to extension to the west. The new broom of the Southern Railway reached Exeter in 1933. Queen Street was provided with new buildings and to mark the event, as well as to stress its geographical advantage, it was renamed Exeter Central. It was the Southern's principal station in the West, but under the Western Region it has undergone progressive downgrading to the role of an intermediate station.

Both views were taken from the bridge which spans the east end of the station, with the camera pointing to the west. The first was one of F. Moore's paintings, based on a photograph. It shows the station about fifty years after its opening, with the down platform extended and widened, and the up platform widened but not extended. Centre roads are provided for various reasons, including the passage of trains not calling at the station and the stabling of rolling stock. The centre roads at Exeter were sometimes used for stabling, but their main use arose from the need to change locomotives, and the provision of banking engines on the incline down to St David's. Locomotives would occupy the centre roads, awaiting the arrival of trains they were to take over or, having left a train, wait for a path to proceed to the engine shed which was opened at Exmouth Junction in 1880. The first view shows two locomotives on the centre road bearing the engine head signals for their trains, and the station pilot locomotive waiting in the siding at the end of the up platform. Of the three semaphore signals two are of the lattice type, but that on the right has a wooden slotted post. The goods sidings and warehouse appear on the right. The reputation of the old station for darkness was partly attributable to the propensity of the overall roof to retain smoke and soot. However, its position on a wooded north facing slope would also have contributed to the lack of light.

The second view was taken from the same bridge, but from a position a little further to the right, about sixty years later. There is evidence of the high period of the station following the rebuilding of 1933, and of the running-down in the 1960s. In 1933 no fundamental alteration was made to the site, and the retaining wall on the left appears in both views. The basic arrangement of two side platforms with centre roads was retained, but the platforms were lengthened, with bays on both up and down sides. The capacity of the up platform was increased by the provision of a scissors crossover joining the platform track to the through road roughly halfway along it, enabling it to be used as two platforms. This increased the capacity of the station to handle trains, and new accommodation was provided for the passengers. Brick buildings, ornamented with stone, were erected alongside a forecourt adjoining Queen Street, the back of which appear to the left of the photograph. At platform level, the overall roof was removed, and replaced by typical Southern canopies. The glass-fronted station nameboards and the electric lighting, shown in the picture, belong to the 1933 rebuilding. Alternative passenger access was given from the bridge from which the photograph was taken, but this was closed as part of the downgrading of the station. Even more drastically, the rather fine booking hall in Queen Street was let, and passengers gained access through the adjoining parcels office. Rationalisation of the track layout began with taking the scissors crossover out of use in 1967, and the centre road on the up side in 1969. The signal box and sidings at the west end of the station were closed in 1970, and also the carriage shed at the east end. In 1971, the year in which the photograph was taken, the goods yard was simplified. The only rolling stock to be seen consists of a Western Region DMU in the up bay, and tankers, wagons and vans in the freight yard. Although the running down of a comparatively modern station is inevitably depressing, it would be hard to justify the maintenance of two main stations in a place the size of Exeter, and the choice of St David's rather than Central was an obvious one.

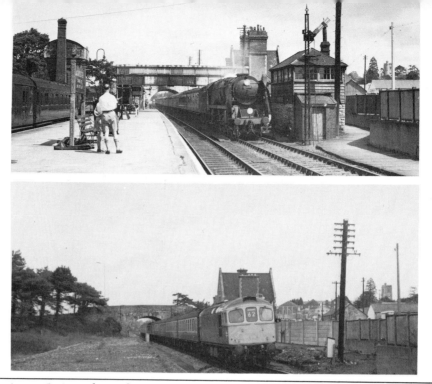

158, 159 Axminster Station, formerly LSWR (SY 292982), on 28 July 1960 and 10 February 1977

The line between Salisbury and Exeter opened throughout in 1860, and served a number of market towns, none of them large and some of them economically stagnant. Axminster, with a population of less than 3000, had lost its famous carpet manufacturers, although it did have small corn and saw mills, a brush factory and an iron foundry. The carpet making was revived in 1937, but Axminster remains the kind of town that might well have lost its railway. In the event, although the days of the Southern's West of England main line have passed, Axminster and places like it, with their restaurant car trains calling roughly every two hours, are better served than many towns in other parts of the country with a comparable traffic potential.

The first view, from the up platform looking in the up direction, was taken three years before the transfer of the Salisbury to Exeter line from the Southern to the Western Region of British Railways. The Exeter train consists of BR Mk1 stock except for the two leading ex-Southern coaches of Maunsell design. The locomotive, rebuilt Merchant Navy class No.35028, was built at Eastleigh Works in 1948 and withdrawn in 1967. Axminster became a junction in 1903 when the branch to Lyme Regis was opened. This crossed over the main line to the west of the station to descend to a terminal at the back of the up platform. After the removal of a spur on the down side in 1915 there was no provision for through running, which was virtually ruled out by the restrictions on the branch. The Maunsell coaches of the branch train are visible on the left. Distinctive features are the water tank, with the

chimney belonging to the boiler and steam pump, and the early LSW signal cabin. Parts of water cranes are visible at the ends of both platforms. Both the starting signals have upper quadrant arms but only one retains its LSW lattice post. The steeply pitched gables and prominent chimneys of the original station buildings appear above the locomotive.

The adaptation of Axminster began in 1965 with the closure of the Lyme Regis line and its platform. In 1967 the signal box and signals, together with all tracks except a single line, were removed. With the passing of steam, the water cranes and the large water tank which supplied them, became redundant. The second view shows what remained on a winter's day early in 1977. The buildings are not greatly changed, although the chimneys have been reduced in height. A surviving telegraph pole and some Southern concrete fencing indicates the site of the signal box. The up platform has lost its asphalt surface and concrete coping but is still discernible. The two trains are in the same position which makes possible a comparison of length. (Although the first view was taken in the summer, there is now no variation in the standard eight coach trains, including restaurant and buffet facilities.) The 1977 view shows the 11.00 from Waterloo to Exeter hauled by Class 33/0 No.33018, built by the Birmingham Railway Wagon and Carriage Co. in 1960. Despite its comparatively austere appearance, it may well be that Axminster illustrates an effective adaptation to present traffic conditions.

160, 161, 162 Colyford Station, formerly LSWR (SY 254926), on 3 August 1958, 6 June 1967 and 23 September 1973

Like most of the East Devon branches, that to Seaton was promoted by an independent company, later absorbed by the LSWR. It was opened in 1868 and had two intermediate stations at Colyton and Colyford. The small town of Colyton was given station buildings and goods facilities, but Colyford never had more than a single platform. It was closed with the rest of the line in 1966. In character it closely resembled White Notley (Photo No.103), but its site is now used in a very different way.

At the north end of the station was a level crossing with the busy A35 road, and the first view was taken from a point just south of the level crossing gates. It shows the maximum development of Colyford. The wooden waiting room and booking office, together with the handsome pre-

fabricated cast iron urinal, belong to the early days of the station; the concrete fencing and waiting shed were added by the Southern Railway, possibly in 1937. However, original iron lamp posts, with a crossbar to support a ladder, survive, with oil lamps *in situ*. The length of the platform would suffice for the normal branch train. The track consists of standard bullhead rail in chairs, but rests on concrete sleepers. The porter, whose bicycle clips may indicate ownership of the adjacent bicycle, seems to be removing a piece of litter from under the seat with his foot.

The second view, taken from the opposite end of the station, shows Colyford just over a year after closure. The track remains intact, as well as the concrete fence and waiting shed, although the latter has suffered from vandalism. The iron urinal remains but the lamp posts have gone. The level crossing gates survive, together with warning notices, and the ground frame from which they were controlled. Other features are the telegraph poles and, beyond the level crossing, a concrete platelayer's hut.

The common feature shown on all three views is the iron urinal which, together with the level crossing gates, establishes the position of the third photograph. Modern Electric Tramways Ltd established a narrow gauge railway for pleasure riding at Eastbourne in 1954. The rolling stock consisted of miniature electric tram cars. When their lease was not renewed they sought a new location. Negotiation was finally completed with British Rail and a terminal was constructed a short distance north of the BR Seaton Station. Narrow gauge track was laid on the old track bed, initially as far as the Colyford level crossing. At first, cars were powered from a battery conveyed on a trolley but later overhead wire, supported by lineside posts, was provided. Public services began in 1971. Photo No.162 shows the first car to convey members of the public from Seaton to Colyford using the overhead wire. A low platform was under construction. Subsequently this has been completed and a second platform added on part of the site of the BR platform. Car No.12, a single deck 8-wheeler, was constructed by MET at Eastbourne in 1966. Extension of the line to Colyton is in progress. Several schemes for adaptation of abandoned routes for pleasure railways have been formulated, with perhaps the Ravenglass & Eskdale the best known; however, the revival of the Seaton branch, including Colyford Station, is one of the most unusual.

163, 164 Woody Bay Station, formerly Lynton and Barnstaple Railway (SS 682463), about 1930 and on 14 April 1963

The Lynton and Barnstaple Railway was built mainly for the benefit of the small North Devon town of Lynton and the neighbouring harbour of Lynmouth. It consisted of about 19 miles of 1 ft 11½ in gauge single track, with passing places. Despite the narrow gauge making sharp curves possible, heavy engineering works were necessary to carry the railway through the hills of North Devon. This line was opened in 1898 but had cost so much that the hopes of the shareholders were dashed. It was sold to the Southern Railway and subsequently closed in 1935. Most of the intermediate stations served small rural communities, but Woody Bay had a hotel and hopes of a growing tourist trade. The station was about a mile and a half from the bay, a short enough distance by the standards of the day. For a line dogged by financial problems, the three station houses built by the company were remarkable buildings, incorporating stone, hanging tiles and roofing slates. The Nüremburg style may indicate the influence of Sir George Newnes – in any event, they were fine period pieces. A particular feature was the extension of the roof over the platform, as a substitute for a separate canopy. The stations were fully signalled, and both point rodding and a semaphore signal are visible. However, the low platforms did represent an economy. In the first view a train for Lynton, hauled by one of the four 2-6-2 tank locomotives, is approaching, awaited by a member of the station staff and four passengers. Already bus competition was draining away traffic.

The second view was taken in pouring rain, which must have been testing the water resistance of the station building. All the ancillary buildings had been removed but the station continued in use as a dwelling with only minor changes. Even the two elaborate chimney pots and the finials on the ridge of the roof had survived. The coping stone of the down platform was shining in the rain. If only the Lynton and Barnstaple could have kept going until the 1950s it would have been a very strong candidate for preservation.

165, 166 Bath, Green Park Station, formerly Midland Railway (ST 745647), on 23 December 1965 and on 16 July 1976

The Midland's line between Bristol and Gloucester was opened in 1844. Bath was connected to it by a branch with a triangular junction at Mangotsfield in 1869, thus securing connection to the Midlands and also an alternative to the GW route to Bristol. In 1874, the Somerset & Dorset opened their route from a junction about half a mile short of the station to join their existing line from Burnham to Wimborne at Evercreech Junction, thus providing Bath with a route to the South. This was not a triangular junction, so that all trains from the Midlands to the South ran in and out of the terminal, which was named Queen Square. The opening of a fine building in a Georgian style in 1870 may have been influenced by the established presence of the GW in the city. After the closure of the S&D in March 1966 there was little hope of the retention of the terminal station, which had been renamed Green Park in 1951. It was closed in August 1966. Traffic to Bath Gas Works continued for some time, but the line from Mangotsfield was finally closed in 1971.

Green Park was little altered and provided an unspoilt example of a station of the high Victorian period. It consisted of two centre roads and two platform roads. The fine train shed remained unchanged and no platforms were added, although there was some lengthening. The first view was taken from the southern platform not long before the closure. Through trains from the Midlands had already been withdrawn, and the photograph shows the 13.10 departure for Templecombe. The train consists of a 3-coach Bulleid set from the Southern Region, with a van, and the locomotive is one of the BR 75XXX class. The number plate has been removed from the smokebox door. The gas lamps are a reminder that the station continued to be lit by gas until its closure.

The second view was taken ten years after closure, from the same position. The most important change is the removal of the rails and the substitution of a blacktop surface to form a car park. Electric light has been substituted for gas, but the train shed is virtually unchanged. In 1977 the future of both the station buildings and the train shed was under consideration, the possibilities including the adaptation of the train shed to form a supermarket. It is worth saving.

6 The Midlands

167, 168 Stoke Works Station, formerly GWR (SO 942665), about 1910 and on 18 July 1976

Stoke Works was unusual, being a GW station on a GW line, but was served by Midland and, later, LMS trains. The Birmingham and Gloucester Railway was opened in 1840, and became part of the Midland in 1846. It was built on Stephenson's principle of making a good line between its terminals, and Worcester was left about 3 miles away to the west. A branch would probably have been built, but in the event the standard gauge Oxford, Worcester and Wolverhampton company constructed a loop line which served the city. The southern section, from Abbots Wood Junction on the B&G, was opened in 1850 and the remainder, from Worcester through Droitwich to a junction adjoining Stoke Works, in 1852. From Norton, three quarters of a mile beyond Abbots Wood Junction, through Worcester to Droitwich the line was shared by Midland trains using the Worcester loop and OW&W trains, as it formed a part of their main line. The famous salt works at Stoke Prior had been opened on the Worcester and Birmingham Canal in 1828, and were served by the B&G Railway from 1840. Some time between 1852 and 1855 the passenger station at Stoke Works on the Worcester loop was opened, and the original station which had been opened on the B&G was retained for goods traffic only. The OW&W Rly. became part of the West Midland Rly. in 1860 and part of the Great Western in 1863. The Midland, and later the LMS, continued to run over the Worcester loop, and in this way the former GW station at Stoke Works was being served by trains of the London Midland Region of BR when it was closed in 1966.

Both views were taken from the northbound platform,

which for the GW was the down platform and for the Midland the up platform. The station itself had no points or signals, those in the photograph being Midland signals worked from a box at Stoke Works Junction. The station name board is of GW pattern and, although not visible in the picture, the fire buckets and clock were marked 'GWR'. The modest wooden buildings, which served as a booking and parcels office, a waiting room and a ladies room, have a GW air about them as have the tiles with which the platforms were paved. The small shelter on the northbound platform is GW in style; the trolley, half visible under the canopy, looks Midland, but the porter standing with his lamps in the six foot way is not wearing clothing which can be readily associated with either company. In the background, beyond the station buildings, the chimneys of the salt works are visible.

The second view was taken after the closure of the station and of the works. The tiles with which the platform was paved have been removed, but a few of the bricks which formed the coping have survived. The best links between the two photographs are the chimney and roof of the dwelling on the right, and one parapet of the bridge which carried the line over a road at the north end of the station. Although still used as part of the main line between Worcester and Birmingham, the section between Droitwich and Stoke Works Junction has been singled. Stoke Works Junction is controlled from the panel box at Gloucester, and the colour light signal protecting the junction may be seen. Stoke Works Station was very closely associated with the works, so their joint demise is not surprising.

As mentioned above, the Oxford, Worcester and Wolverhampton Railway was opened in stages, the section from Wolvercot Junction, near Oxford, to Evesham being completed in 1853. The Cotswold market town of Chipping Norton was connected by a branch line from Kingham in 1855. It remained a dead end until 1887 when it became part of the Banbury to Cheltenham Direct line. For a while Chipping Norton was served by long-distance express trains, a service from Newcastle to Cardiff and Barry being inaugurated in 1907. For instance, in 1939 the Ports-to-Ports express stopped at Chipping Norton in the southbound direction at 16.09, and northbound at 12.05. However, in order to be allowed to join or leave the train, passengers had to be travelling at least as far as Rugby or Gloucester. This train was not restored after the Second World War, and soon the run-down of services began. The last through passenger train from Kingham to Banbury ran in 1951, and Chipping Norton reverted to its branch line status. This lasted until passenger services were withdrawn in 1962, to be followed by freight in 1964.

The first view was taken in the spring of 1962. At this time a number of trains worked through from Cheltenham to Chipping Norton, but the timetable showed separate services between Kingham and Cheltenham and between Kingham and Chipping Norton. The photograph shows the 16.53 departure from Chipping Norton, drawing into the southbound platform. This consisted of the coaches which had formed the 16.00 from Kingham, the locomotive having run round its train. The train was hauled by 51XX class 2-6-2T No.4163, at that time allocated to Gloucester M.P.D. (85B). It was built at Swindon Works in 1948 and withdrawn in 1962. The two Great Western coaches were both side corridor brakes, one second class and one composite (Nos.W1783 W and W6543 W). When the original branch was connected to the new line to Kings Sutton, south of Banbury, the junction at Chipping Norton was short of the original terminal, and a through station was opened at the same time as the new line. (Although the footbridge carried a plate inscribed 'Arrol Bros. Germiston Iron Works. Glasgow, 1886'.) The goods shed and the engine shed remained unmoved but the signalling was altered with new boxes being added, one on the southbound platform and the other at the Kingham end of the goods yard. The first casualty was the engine shed, closed in 1922, followed by the West Signal Box in 1929. A period of stability followed until 1956, five years after the withdrawal of the Kingham to Banbury passenger service. At this time the signalling was simplified and the connections to the east end of the goods yard were removed. The canopies were removed from the platform side of the main buildings and from the waiting room on the northbound side. This was the situation recorded by the first photograph in 1962. Despite the onset of withdrawal, the red brick buildings and the timber signal cabin with its decorative barge-boards have not been altered greatly. The imminence of tea time is indicated by the fireman with his tea can, his beret and bicycle clips being part of the informal uniform of locomotive firemen in the early sixties.

After the end of the passenger service, the private sidings to the gas works and the tweed factory were closed, and finally in 1964 the railway to Chipping Norton was closed. The second photograph, from 1976, includes a number of links, the most striking being the platforms. Also visible are the road bridge and some of the trees; the site of the signal box is shown by the break in the platform face, once occupied by rods and wires. It now requires a great deal of imagination to visualize the Ports-to-Ports express, with a 4-6-0 of the Manor class, making its daily call at Chipping Norton.

171, 172, 173, 174 Cheddington Station, formerly LNWR (SP 356089), about 1930, on 20 July 1976, 4 August 1949 and 20 July 1976

The London and Birmingham Railway was opened in 1838. Stephenson's policy was to adopt the optimum alignment between two terminals but to provide branch lines to the more important towns on either side of the line. The first of the branches was to Aylesbury, and this was opened, together with a junction station at Cheddington, in 1839. The junction faced in the Birmingham direction, and there was no intention to run through-trains from London, so a station for changing onto the Aylesbury train or shunting through-coaches was necessary. But for this, the London and Birmingham would not have opened a station at a village the size of Cheddington. Extra tracks were added on the up or east side, a third in 1859 and a fourth in 1876, followed by a rebuilding of the station. Like St Albans, Aylesbury came to be served by three companies, being reached by the GW in 1863 and by the Metropolitan in 1892. With such elaborate provision it is not surprising that BR withdrew the former LNWR passenger service from Cheddington in 1953, and the branch was closed to all traffic in 1963. After 124 years Cheddington ceased to be a junction. However, electrification of the main line was already in progress and in 1966 Cheddington enjoyed an improved service of electric trains. Closure to goods occurred in 1963, but passenger traffic increased and new buildings

were constructed.

Photos 171 and 172 were taken from the road bridge at the south end of the station. At the beginning of 1923, the LNWR became part of the new London, Midland and Scottish Railway, but although the first view was taken in LMS days, there had been no appreciable changes since the grouping. For instance, the tall posts of the home signals, with their co-acting arms, visible either above or below the bridge from which the view was taken, are typical of the LNW. The up starter on the main line uses the same post as the home signal on the down relief line, but a separate post is provided for the up starter on the relief line. The telegraph posts are a prominent feature on both sides of the line. Because of the extent to which the platforms are staggered, a wooden footwalk, presumably reserved for the use of staff, forms an extension to the centre island platform. The buildings, which appear between the tall signal posts, had replaced those of 1839, but were in roughly the same position. They consisted of a booking office and waiting rooms on a single storey; staff dwellings, including the station master's house, were separate. Typical LNW housing for their staff appears on the left of the photograph.

The second photograph, No.172, was taken from a little further to the east on the same bridge about forty-six years

later. The most striking change is the provision of the gantries and overhead wiring for the 25kV electrification. The LNW signal posts have been replaced by metal posts with colour light signals, two of which are in roughly the positions once occupied by the up starters. With 100 mph trains, crossing of the tracks by staff is discouraged, and although the wooden footwalk forming an extension to the centre island platform has survived, the two wooden crossings joining it to the up and down platform have been removed. The chaired track has been replaced by continuous welded rail, but the small ballast bin on the up side appears in both photographs. Of particular significance are the parked cars of commuters in the station yard, but perhaps the most striking development at Cheddington is the conversion of the staff houses into commuter's residences.

Photos 173 and 174 were taken from the down side platform, both showing express trains rushing through the station. Although photograph No.173 was taken shortly after nationalisation, apart from the train and the station nameboard, everything in the photograph belongs to the late Victorian period of the LNWR. Particularly characteristic are the station building and the blue tiles with which the platform is paved. Gas lamps are shown, both on posts and suspended from the canopy of the

building. The footbridge is roofed to protect passengers, and cowls are attached to it to give protection from the exhaust of steam locomotives. The right hand side of the platform was used by the Aylesbury branch train. In the foreground is a modest station garden, reflecting the more favourable ratio between available staff and amount of railway work to be done which prevailed at the time. The down express, consisting of LMS coaches, is hauled by No.45540. This was built at Crewe Works in 1933 as Baby Scot class No.5540 'Sir Robert Turnbull'. It was rebuilt in 1947 and withdrawn in 1963.

Photograph No.174 was taken from almost the same position, after the closure of the Aylesbury branch and the electrification of the main line. The station buildings have been replaced for the second time, and electric lighting has been installed. The platform paving remains unchanged, but the bridge has lost its roof and its cowls. The telegraph line has gone underground. By the time this photograph was taken the practice of carrying train numbers on the front of trains had ceased, and to avoid confusion the locomotive shows four zeros. With the train passing at about 100 mph, identity of the locomotive was not established. Wayside stations on main lines have suffered a high casualty rate, but Cheddington has been saved by its growing commuter traffic.

Two important branch lines, which together formed a useful cross-country route, left the LNW main line at Bletchley, one going east to Cambridge and the other to the west, for Oxford and Banbury. The Oxford and Banbury lines forked at a junction 9½ miles from Bletchley. Banbury was reached in 1850, but, owing to unforeseen delays, LNW trains did not reach Oxford until 1851. There was no station at the junction. As mentioned previously, the GW reached Aylesbury from Princess Risborough in 1863, and the Aylesbury and Buckingham Railway was authorised in 1860. After rejection by the LNWR it was operated by the GW, with a northern terminal at the junction of the Oxford and Banbury lines. To reach Buckingham, which was an intermediate station on the LNW Banbury line, passengers had to change trains, and so a station was opened at this isolated spot in 1868. As there was no clear association with any settlement it was named Verney Junction, after Sir Harry Verney, a local landowner with railway interests, and this became one of the few stations to bear a personal name. In 1891, the Aylesbury and Buckingham was taken over by the Metropolitan Railway as part of their thrust to the north, and was connected to their main system in 1892. They doubled the line, and at the beginning of 1897 commenced to run through-trains from Verney Junction to Baker Street. Although the traffic potential of the line north of Aylesbury was decidedly limited, the service continued as the furthest outpost of the Baker Street empire. However, in 1933 the Metropolitan was absorbed by London Transport and, not surprisingly, in 1936 the passenger service between Quainton Road and Verney Junction was withdrawn. The line however was retained as a useful link between the Met. & GC Joint and the Bletchley to Oxford line until 1947. (By this time the wartime link at Calvert served this function.) The passenger service between Banbury and Buckingham was withdrawn in 1961, between Buckingham and Verney Junction in 1964, and in 1966 the line was closed to all traffic. The Bletchley to Oxford passenger service ceased at the end of 1967 and Verney Junction was closed. However, the line remains open to freight traffic, although the goods depot at Verney Junction closed in 1964.

Both photographs were taken from the footbridge that provided access to both platforms. The booking office was latterly situated on the island platform, one face of which was used by the Oxford and Banbury trains and the other by the Metropolitan. The first view shows an LMS train, probably the 18.14 departure for Bletchley, having left from the eastbound platform, with a Metropolitan train, the 18.20 for Baker Street, at the Metropolitan platform. This train is headed by No.107, a 4-4-4 tank locomotive of

the H class, built by Kerr, Stuart for the Metropolitan in 1921. This was purchased by the LNER in 1937, became their No.6419 and was withdrawn in 1943. Steam haulage gave place to an electric locomotive at Rickmansworth, and the stock was dual-heated. The coach is one of the last of the series incorporating teak, delivered in 1927 and 1929. Typical Metropolitan features such as the round-topped doors and the bars on the windows are visible. The lines to the right of the platform were operated by the Metropolitan and GC Joint Committee and, like the train, the signals and signal box on this side are characteristic of the Metropolitan, although the concrete post of the starting signal was a little unusual. The water tower belonged to the Met. but the station house on the extreme right was LNWR property. The up starter, not yet put back after the departure of the Bletchley train, and the down bracketed home signals are all typical of the LNWR. The junction of the Oxford and Banbury lines was at the west end of the station, and it does seem rather strange that the junction signal should be at the east end. The photograph shows the signal pulled off for the Oxford line. The platform has oil lamps and a nameboard announcing 'Verney Junction. Junction of Oxford and Banbury Branches and Metropolitan Lines'.

The second view was taken after the abandonment of the Metropolitan service. The physical junction between the LNW and the Met. & GC Joint adjoined that of the Oxford and Banbury lines, just west of the station. The wagons stored in the former Metropolitan sidings must have used that connection. When the second photograph was taken, the Bletchley to Buckingham service was being maintained by two single-unit railcars. One of these cars is shown departing at 13.46 for Bletchley, after its arrival from Buckingham. All the LNW and Metropolitan signals have been removed. The up starter has been replaced by a metal post and upper quadrant arm in the same position, but the junction signal has been moved to the junction at the west end of the station. On the island platform are the rather sad remains of a station garden, which included not only flower beds, but also a sun dial and a birds' nesting box, both of which are visible. The lamps show signs of neglect, although the posts survive (one of them forms part of a group comprising the nesting box, the post-war station name board and some oil drums). It is surprising that this remote station survived in the fields of Buckinghamshire as late as 1967. Even more remarkable is the fact that for many years it was possible to travel from Verney Junction to Baker Street in the luxury of one of the Metropolitan's two 1910 Pullman Cars, 'Mayflower' or 'Galatea'.

177, 178 The top of Hopton Incline, formerly LNWR (SK 252547), on 10 August 1953 and 23 June 1972

The Cromford and High Peak Railway was part of the canal system rather than the railway network. It belonged to the canal age, being authorised in 1825 and opened throughout in 1831. Because of the difficulties of canal construction over the pervious limestone of the Peak District, a railway was built to connect the Peak Forest to the Cromford Canal. It was a typical line of the canal and horse railway era, with inclined planes worked by stationary steam engines separated by horse-worked levels. With the passing of the years, steam locomotives replaced horses on the levels, and also began to work up all but the steepest of the rope worked inclines. At both ends of the line connections were made with the railway network. At the Cromford end a connection was made with the Midland in 1853. The LNWR leased the C&HPR, finally absorbing it in 1887. Considerable lengths at the western end were closed in the 1890s when the LNW opened their line from Buxton to Ashbourne, using parts of the C&HPR north of Parsley Hay. On the 'unimproved' section between Parsley Hay and Cromford, closure came in stages. When the Middleton Incline was closed in 1963, the line was divided into two parts. Traffic between Parsley Hay and the top of the incline finally ended in 1967.

One of the inclines on which locomotives replaced rope working with a stationary steam engine was at Hopton.

This was converted in 1877. It was 457 yards long and after conversion rose successively at 1 in 60, 1 in 30, 1 in 20, 1 in 14 and then eased to 1 in 470. This was the steepest gradient worked by locomotives on BR. Trains ascending were limited to five loaded wagons or seven empties, and achieved the summit by taking a run at it. The first view shows a train approaching the top gradient post at the conclusion of a successful ascent. The locomotive is a former North London Railway 0-6-0 tank locomotive No.58856. This was built at Bow Works to a design of 1879, and was not withdrawn until 1975. If locomotives had feelings, the transition from the teaming environs of North London to the windswept heights of the High Peak line must have proved traumatic. Although the C&HPR had had no regular passenger services for many years, it did not escape the attention of the organisers of special trains, and the present writer had the experience of riding up Hopton Incline in a train of brake vans on 25 September 1955. The second view, taken from the same viewpoint as the first, shows the incline without railway track. The mound on the left, which appears in both photographs, marks the site of the stationary steam engine, put out of use in 1877. Even with no rails, it requires no great effort of the imagination to visualise generations of small tank engines just breasting the top of the incline.

179, 180 Millers Dale Station, formerly Midland Railway (SK 137733), on 24 June 1933 and 19 July 1976

The Midland main line to Manchester was completed in stages. In 1849 a branch was opened from Ambergate on the Derby to Rotherham line as far as Rowsley. This remained the terminus until the route was extended towards Manchester. The new main line joined Rowsley to an existing line at New Mills and, with its very heavy engineering works, was not completed until 1867. However, the eastern section, through Bakewell and Millers Dale, with a branch to Buxton, was opened in 1863. Buxton Junction was the obvious position for the junction station, but the site was somewhat inaccessible and extremely difficult from a constructional viewpoint. (In fact two small platforms, known as Blackwell Halt, were provided at this point, with a footpath to Blackwell village and access from some Midland Railway houses.) Millers Dale Station was opened about 1¼ miles east of the junction near Blackwell Mill on a level stretch of line. Because of the lack of any nearby settlement, Blackwell Mill was considered as a name for the station, but Millers Dale, reflecting the number of mill sites on this part of the River Wye, was chosen instead. Originally the station consisted of through platforms with a bay for the Buxton branch, but in 1905 an enlarged version was completed. The up platform became an island and a new platform was added, thus serving four through-tracks instead of two. Just east of the station the Wye was crossed by a viaduct, and it was necessary to construct a second viaduct when

the station was widened. The Buxton branch closed at the same time as Millers Dale Station and the main line, in 1967.

The first view was taken just after the arrival of a down Manchester express, with passengers transferring to the local train for Buxton. This consists of Johnson 0-4-4 tank locomotive No. 1421 with Midland compartment coaches. The wooden buildings on this platform were not rebuilt when the station was 'widened' in 1905. The two lamp glasses of the oil lamps are clearly visible. The telegraph line may be seen beyond the engine run-round loop. In the background, the limestone quarries are a prominent feature but the lime kilns, which were served by a private siding, are obscured.

The second view was taken from the west end of the station and shows all three platforms. From left to right they are the up main, the central island platform serving the up and down relief lines, and the southern platform for the down main and the Buxton branches. Many of the buildings on the up main platform survive although they are no longer in railway use and are not on the photograph. However nothing remains on the other two platforms. The site of the quarries and lime kilns which forms a background to both photographs has become overgrown. Unless the site is used for another purpose, the station which once accommodated elegant passengers, changing for Buxton, will soon be similarly obscured.

Lincoln Central is one of the small number of major provincial stations of the 1840s which retain their original buildings with only minor alterations. It was opened on the Great Northern's Lincolnshire loop line in 1848, four years before the completion of their main line to the North via Grantham. The Midland had reached Lincoln with their line from Nottingham via Newark in 1846, which may have provided an extra incentive for the GN to construct prestigious buildings. While the Lincolnshire loop only had a brief reign as the GN main route to the North, Lincoln Station became the focal point for a number of other lines. The Manchester, Sheffield and Lincolnshire Railway, later the Great Central, ran in from the west via Retford, and from the north-east from Grimsby via Market Rasen. From 1881, the Great Eastern reached Lincoln over what became the GN and GE joint line from March to Doncaster via Spalding. In 1867 the GN opened a connecting line from Sincil Junction, about $\frac{1}{4}$ mile east of the station, to Honington on the Sleaford to Barkston line. Finally, in 1896, the Lancashire, Derbyshire and East Coast line joined the western approaches to Lincoln at Pye Wipe Junction. There were therefore, a maximum of six lines converging on the GN station at Lincoln; going in a clockwise direction, there was firstly the original GN line to Boston of 1848, then the GN & GE Joint to Spalding, the GN to Honington, the LD & EC to Chesterfield, the GN (later the GN & GE) to Gainsborough and lastly the GC to Grimsby. (The GC line to Retford diverged from the GN & GE to Gainsborough at Sykes Junction, about 8 miles from the city.) All these lines contributed passenger traffic to Lincoln Station. However, the GN & GE route, with its heavy coal traffic, included a by-pass line passing round the south of the city, which was used by through freight trains. By 1977 three out of the six lines mentioned above had lost their passenger services. The service to the LD & EC was withdrawn in 1955, that on the route via Honington in 1962, while the service on the Boston line went in two stages. Regular services to Firsby used the line as far as Coningsby Junction until 1970, but the remainder of the line on to Boston saw its last passenger train in 1963. At the present time, virtually all the trains serving Lincoln Central use the former GN & GE Joint line, the Sheffield service running via Gainsborough, together with the March to Doncaster service. One train a day runs to Grimsby, but normally the service on the Grimsby line operates from the former Midland station.

Both views were taken from a footbridge looking to the west. Footbridge provision was generous at Lincoln, and a second, covered footbridge is visible at the west end of the station. A crossing for members of the staff joins the ends of the platforms, and a level crossing with a public road is visible beyond. The top of the Great Northern Hotel appears above the footbridge. This was contemporary with the station and was an early example of a hotel linked to the railway. Unlike the station, its architectural style owed much to the eighteenth century. Perhaps the most striking feature of the station itself was its overall roofs. Both the columns and the horizontal beams were made of iron, with a high degree of decoration. The GN style may be contrasted with roof at St Albans, LNWR (No.127). The roof consisted of Welsh slates with louvres let into a clerestory type ridge to assist smoke dispersal. The view only shows the main platform and the through roads; there were four bay platforms at the east end of the right hand (e.g. eastbound) platform, and two through platforms, on the left. LNE coaches occupy the main, westbound platform, and a permanent way engineer's train, apparently running to the east, nevertheless occupies the westbound, through track. A K1 class locomotive is entering the eastbound platform road. This was No.61948, built by the North British Loco Co. in 1935 and withdrawn in 1962. Only two signals are visible. First, the starter signal for the westbound through track: this was an upper quadrant of LNE design, suspended from a bracket below and to the right of the top of the metal lattice post. The second signal is the ground signal controlling the use of the crossover, near the end of the platforms. Even for a station where virtually all trains stopped, the track ballast seems unusually dirty.

The second view was taken about 21 years later. The obvious change is the removal of the overall roofs, and their replacement by canopies supported by steel columns mounted on the platforms. The foundations of the old roofs show faintly, especially to the left of the brake van in the foreground. Again, a permanent way engineer's train appears, but in the second view it is diesel-hauled and proceeding to the west on the westbound track. The buildings are virtually unchanged, but minor developments include the provision of fluorescent lighting, while 'Brute' trolleys are to be seen on the eastbound platform. The Great Northern Hotel has been replaced by a new building. Although the ballast is cleaner, there is no apparent change in the track layout or signalling. (In fact, some of the platforms not shown on either of the views have been put out of use.) Presumably there have been some changes in the signalling arrangements as a white flattened diamond, indicating exemption from Rule 55, has been added to the signal post. However, from an architectural and historical point of view, the most important thing about Lincoln Central are its very fine Tudor-style buildings, and these are well preserved.

183, 184 Sutton Bridge, formerly Midland and Great Northern Joint Committee (TF 480210), on 9 August 1958 and 21 January 1977

Sutton Bridge originated as a landing place on the River Nene about 7 miles downstream from Wisbech. In 1850 a road swing-bridge, designed by Robert Stephenson, was opened across the river. In 1862 Sutton Bridge was reached by the Norwich and Spalding Railway, which started from Spalding and terminated on the west bank of the river. The N&S was financially exhausted, and the crossing of the Nene and the extension to the east was carried out by the Lynn and Sutton Bridge company in 1864. Owing to lack of money, the latter company did not build a bridge in line with the Norwich and Spalding, but adapted the existing road bridge to take a railway track. This necessitated a junction short of the original terminal, and an S bend to reach the road bridge, which was about 300 yards north of the intended site for the railway bridge. A new station was opened by the Lynn and Sutton Bridge company, and in 1866 both companies were absorbed into the Midland and Eastern Railway. Also, in 1866, the Peterborough, Wisbech and Sutton Bridge joined the N&S, a short distance to the west of Sutton Bridge station. With regard to ownership, in 1883 the Midland and Eastern joined other companies to form the Eastern and Midlands Railway, which in 1893 became the Midland and Great Northern Joint Railway. At Sutton Bridge the pressure of traffic on the 1850 bridge increased so much as to necessitate the construction of a new bridge, with separate decks for road and rail. This was located south of the old bridge, so the rail approaches at each end were diverted, and the passenger station was re-sited accordingly. The new steel bridge was opened in 1897. In 1902 the railway company were freed from the obligation to maintain the approach roads, and accordingly ceased to collect tolls for use of the road carriageway. Some years earlier, in 1881, a dock was opened at Sutton Bridge, but engineering difficulties were encountered, and the only port traffic passed over a riverside quay. Apart from this the main freight traffic was agricultural; in particular, soft fruits and market garden produce. This was sufficient to justify the retention of the line to Spalding for freight after the closure, in 1959, of the M&GN to passenger traffic. However, complete closure followed in 1965.

The first view was taken from the east end of the platform. The excursion train, returning from Great Yarmouth, is signalled for the Peterborough line. As explained above, the bridge carried both road and rail traffic. Newcastle High Level Bridge provides an example of segregation at different levels, but the Cross Keys Bridge at Sutton provided horizontal separation, as with the bridge on the LCDR Sheerness branch. Between the two signal boxes shown – the station box to the left of the locomotive, and the East box visible at the other end of the bridge – a single track was provided, and a tablet was issued for its use. In the photograph, the fireman's arm is extended, with the ring with its pouch containing the tablet ready for delivery onto the curved bar from which it will be collected by the signalman. One of the features of interest in this view is the mixture of railway company styles included. For instance, the signal cabins are of the Midland style but the somersault signals are typically Great Northern. The lamp case which appears on earlier photographs on the post at the end of the platform has been replaced by a shade with a strong resemblance to the style favoured by the Southern Railway. The gradient and mileposts are characteristic of the M&GN. The locomotive, No.43086 was a 2-6-0 of LMS design, built at Darlington Works in 1950 and withdrawn in 1964. The leading coach is also of LMS design, followed by a coach from the LNER. Details, such as the level crossing gates, are visible, but dominating the background is the bridge itself. The control tower is perched on the swinging span.

The second view was taken after the removal of the railway and the conversion of the bridge to a dual-carriageway arrangement in 1963, with the deck constructed to take the railway being re-used for road transport. This is not quite a reversal of the situation when a railway track was added to the roadway on the 1850 bridge. Both the control tower with its navigation lights, and the bridge itself, provide links between the two views. But there is almost nothing left to act as a reminder of the Midland and Great Northern Railway, who built the bridge.

7 North of England

185, 186, 187 Crewe, formerly LNWR (SJ 710549), about 1900, on 29 July 1955 and 18 August 1965

Crewe was a small settlement on the Cheshire plain until the coming of the railway. The Grand Junction was opened from Birmingham to a junction with the Liverpool and Manchester in 1837, and a station was opened at Crewe. There was also a small shed for a pilot locomotive, and Lord Crewe opened what is usually acknowledged to be the first railway hotel, now the 'Crewe Arms'. The position of Crewe as a major junction followed the opening of the lines to Holyhead via Chester and to Manchester at the north end, and to Shrewsbury and Stoke at the south end. The great railway works commenced production in 1843. The first major rebuilding of the station was completed in 1867, and the last took place between 1896 and 1906. Other changes have included the installation of power signalling, and the construction of a new building alongside the road above the platforms. Electrification on the 25kV overhead system reached Crewe in 1960, when electric trains began to run between Manchester and Crewe as the first stage of the London Midland main line scheme. This was completed, north to Liverpool and south to London and Birmingham, in 1965. Crewe remained a railhead for the electric haulage of trains until 1974, when electrification was completed between London and Glasgow. Electrification and dieselisation have made a considerable impact in both the running sheds and the works, but Crewe remains one of the principal railway centres in Britain.

The first two views were taken looking to the north from a footbridge demolished in connection with electrification. The first, published by the LNWR as a postcard in January 1905, shows the arrangement of tracks before the major alterations were completed in 1906. The Grand Junction had been extended by a succession of companies until, in 1848, both Edinburgh and Glasgow were reached by rail. The London and North Western was formed in 1846 and became the owner of Crewe Station and the operator of the trains to the north. The five running lines shown were normally used as follows, looking from left to right: down freight, up freight, down main, up main, up relief. The signals for the up main lines are visible. The line to Chester diverges to the left, and that to Manchester is on the right. The former was opened in 1840 and the latter in 1842, but neither occupies its original alignment. In the foreground is the crossing from the freight lines over the main lines, used by goods trains for the Manchester direction. The major alterations at the turn of the century eliminated this obstructive crossing by the expensive expedient of running the freight lines underground. The signalling was mechanical, and of particular interest is the bracket signal for the up Chester line, with arms in slotted posts, separate from the spectacles. The original works are shown between the Chester and Grand Junction lines. Of the six vertical features on the skyline, five are chimneys and the sixth is a church tower, reflecting the growth of housing related to the works. (Owing to the presence of Lord Crewe's estate on the east side, virtually all the Victorian development was west of the main line.) The bridge in the left foreground carried an 18 inch gauge railway, connecting the station with the works.

The second photograph shows the view in the 1950s.

Power signalling has been installed and Crewe North SB appears in the angle between the Chester and Grand Junction lines. Much of the original works remains but the bridge carrying the narrow gauge railway has been demolished. Crewe North Engine Shed occupies the left background. A small depot was established on this site in 1851. This was replaced by a larger shed in 1865/1866, which underwent further extension in the 1896–1906 rebuilding period. (Some relief was provided by the opening of Crewe South Shed in 1896.) Skyline features include two chimneys, the church tower and the top of the Crewe North coaling tower. The long line of coal wagons are almost certainly bringing in supplies for the engine sheds. Three steam locomotives may be seen – an LMS Pacific standing outside the shed, an LMS 2-6-4 tank locomotive on the extreme left and an LMS Standard mixed traffic on the two coaches in the foreground. These two coaches – one former LNW and one LMS – both in BR 'plum and spilt milk' livery, were running through from Plymouth to Glasgow. At Crewe they were backed onto the down 'Midday Scot', when it was standing in platform 2.

The third view was taken from platform 2, after the demolition of the footbridge from which the other photographs were taken. After the rebuilding of 1896/1906,

Crewe consisted of three island platforms, with bays. Normally the western island served down main line trains, the central island was used for up traffic, and the eastern was used by other up trains not terminating, and therefore unable to use the bays. The photograph was taken during the period when trains going north of the Mersey changed from electric to diesel traction at Crewe. The 10.35 had been hauled from Euston by a Class 85 locomotive, then numbered E3084, now No.85029, built at Doncaster Works in 1964. The locomotive shown replacing it at 13.45 was Class 47 D1843, built at Crewe in 1965 (present number, 47193). The leading coach has the round windows at the ends which were a feature of one of the LMS designs. Crewe North Shed closed to steam in 1965, but at the time of the third view retained a few steam locomotives. With steam, electric and diesel locomotives all to be seen, it is not surprising that the seated train spotter thought it worthwhile to bring his sandwiches with him. But knowledge of Crewe is not confined to generations of train-spotters. It is one of the few stations to be celebrated in music hall song; 'Oh! Mr Porter', with its delineation of the young lady who wished to go to Birmingham and was taken on to Crewe, is part of the national heritage.

188, 189, 190 Preston Station, formerly LNWR and LYR (SD 535288), on 21 August 1965, 11 June 1973 and 31 August 1976

Preston, with its port and industries, being both a cultural centre and the county town of Lancashire, has never been a railway town like Crewe. Nevertheless, its station was for some years an important staging point on the West Coast Main Line, and it has been a major junction for nearly 140 years. The Northern Union Railway was opened between Wigan and a terminal in Preston in 1838. In 1840 the Lancaster and Preston Junction was opened, joining the Northern Union just south of its terminal station. At Crewe the junctions adjoin the station, but at Preston they are scattered over several

miles. They vary from important junctions, such as those serving Blackpool and Liverpool, to those serving lines partially closed, such as that to Longridge. In 1846 the Northern Union was leased jointly to the LNW and Lancashire and Yorkshire companies, and in 1850 they built a through station roughly on the present site. This was replaced by the centre island platform of the existing station in 1880, and its outer faces, now numbered 3 and 4, are the normal stopping places for down and up main line trains. However, additional island platforms were added on both sides, the present 1/2 and 5/6, plus an

123

annexe used by the trains for East Lancashire. Relief lines were provided on the west side, from which a steeply-graded single line branch ran down to the docks. The important development in recent years has been the electrification of the West Coast Main Line, completed in 1974. Rationalisation has brought about the closure and subsequent demolition of the East Lancashire platforms; the displaced trains now use platforms 1 and 2.

All three photographs were taken from the centre island platform looking to the north, and all show up express trains on the main line. The first was taken on a wet day in August, with the platform and chaired track shining in the rain. No.70020 'Mercury' was leaving on a London train. This locomotive, which belonged to the BR Brittania class, was built at Crewe in 1951 and withdrawn in 1967. The overall roof of the 1880 station is visible above the modern canopy which protects the extended platform. The roof of the platform for the East Lancashire trains shows above the prefabricated office. Sidings with buffer stops made from old rails are roughly parallel to the East Lancashire line, and contain coaching stock, including an LMS coach with a round window.

When the second photograph was taken, about eight years later, electrification work was in progress. The East Lancashire platform appears, but some of the sidings have been removed, and the space has been used for relief roads for up traffic. On the platform 'Brutes' have replaced the traditional trolleys. The Birmingham train standing at the platform with the reporting number 1 M 24 is hauled by a Class 47 diesel electric locomotive.

The third view, taken about eleven years later than the first, shows electric operation in action. The train shown is the 17.13 to London, hauled by Class 86 electric locomotive No.86225. This was built at Doncaster Works in 1965. By 1976, trains had ceased to carry their reporting numbers, and so the indicator shows four zeros. On the relief line No.86216 waits with a parcels train to follow the express. This certainly demonstrates the use to which the relief tracks are put, but it obscures the site from which the East Lancashire platform has been removed. As explained, the East Lancashire trains now run from the opposite side of the station. However, although this service continues, local traffic has declined while the main line has developed. Because of this Preston retains its atmosphere as one of the most impressive stations of the North.

191, 192, 193 Sankey Viaduct, formerly LNWR (SS 590890), a contemporary drawing, and two photographs of 30 August 1976

There is disagreement about the rival claims of the Stockton and Darlington and the Liverpool and Manchester Railways to mark the transition from the horse to the steam railway. However, with its conveyance of the general public and its methods of operation, the Liverpool and Manchester has a strong case. About 30 miles of line between Liverpool (Crown Street) and Manchester (Liverpool Road) were opened in 1830. There were a number of major engineering works, among them the viaduct which carried the line over the Sankey valley. This valley was followed by the Sankey Canal of 1757, and, comparable to the claims of the S&D and the L&M for

primacy as railways, the Sankey and the Bridgewater both have claims to being the first artificial inland waterway or canal. It is certainly not unreasonable to regard this historic site as the crossing point of the first railway over the first canal. Unfortunately the canal was closed in 1963, and the section near the viaduct was filled in during 1974. The railway viaduct however, continues in use as part of the main route across Northern England.

The first view is taken from an LNW official postcard which reproduced a drawing by Thomas Talbot Bury. Bury was commissioned to produce engravings in aquatints, which Rudolf Ackermann published for the L&MR. Like many pictures of the time, Bury's were accurate in detail, but tend to exaggerate the scale of their subjects. Thus his view of the viaduct from the south side provides a very accurate presentation of the nine arches, constructed of brick with stone facings, and of the abutments with their wing walls of brick. On the bridge is a typical L&M passenger train and, on the canal, a Mersey flat is sailing by.

The first photograph was taken from as near as possible

to Bury's viewpoint on a very misty morning in late summer. Comparison indicates a close similarity in the details, but Bury's arches look much taller. In fact, the viaduct is 25 feet wide, the arches have a 50 foot span, and the crown of the third arch was about 60 feet above the surface of the canal. (This gave room for Mersey flats with sail hoisted.) It suggests that Bury did give a slightly exaggerated impression of the height of the viaduct in relation to the width of the spans. As mentioned above, the viaduct is virtually unchanged but the canal has been filled in.

The third view was taken from the north side, with the Sankey sugar factory visible through the arches. From this angle only seven of the nine arches are shown, and this makes the viaduct appear taller in relation to its length. By way of contrast to the steam hauled L&M train in Bury's print, the photograph shows an Inter-City diesel multiple-unit train. The Sankey Viaduct is remarkable as an early example of a major railway structure, which has survived with little change.

EXCURSION PLATFORM.

194, 195 Euston Road Station, Morecambe, formerly LNWR (SD 436643), about 1906 and on 31 August 1976

There is a close relationship between railways and Victorian seaside resorts, but when the North Western Railway, later absorbed by the Midland, first opened its line to Morecambe in 1848 its initial aim was to establish a packet station. However, a seaside resort did develop, and when, in 1864, the LNWR opened their branch from the West Coast Main Line at Hest Bank, they had seaside traffic in mind. Initially the junction faced north, but in 1888 a spur was opened permitting through running from the south. In the same year new station buildings were constructed. An important development was the addition of a short spur from a point just short of the LNW station to the Midland line. Thus, when in 1958 the former LNW station was closed, trains could run through to the former Midland station, with its site almost on the seafront. However, summer excursion traffic was still heavy enough to necessitate diversions into the closed station, which was not finally abandoned until 1963.

For much of the year, all the traffic at the LNW Morecambe Station could be handled at the side platform adjoining the station buildings. However, to cope with summer excursion traffic two additional platforms were constructed, giving an additional four platform faces. The first view was taken on the excursion platform nearest to the main platform, shortly after the arrival of a train of

L&Y coaches. (Presumably the excursion emanated from the L&YR.) The gaslit compartment coaches would be typical of the rolling stock provided for this type of train. It must be admitted however that the passengers, including the uniformed school boy, appear rather elegant for day excursionists. However, the time – about ten in the morning – would be normal. At this period one would have expected the photographer to receive rather more attention than a side glance from the schoolboy, and particularly from the waistcoated porter, who is walking away along the edge of the platform. With their limited use, excursion platforms were somewhat bare, and the only visible features are gas lamps and the station nameboard. (The distinctive names, Promenade and Euston Road, were only used for the Morecambe stations after the formation of the LMS.) On the right of the photograph, alongside the main platform, LNW coaches are visible.

The second view was taken about seventy years later, after the closure of the station. The surviving features which link the two views are the platform and the houses, virtually unchanged, in the background. There is little to remind one of the generations of day excursionists who trod the platform at the beginning of a memorable day by the sea.

126

196, 197 Manchester Piccadilly, formerly LNW and GC Railways (SJ 849978), on 14 August 1953 and 29 August 1976

A main terminal station, named London Road until 1960, was opened in 1842 to accommodate the trains of the Manchester & Birmingham and the Sheffield, Ashton-under-Lyne & Manchester Railways. In 1846 the M&B became part of the LNW, and in 1847 the SA&M was merged into the Manchester, Sheffield and Lincolnshire, later the Great Central Railway. The Manchester South Junction and Altrincham Railway was opened from the small town of Altrincham in Cheshire to its own station, alongside London Road, in 1849. It crossed inner Manchester on an impressive 224 arch viaduct. The MSJ&A was always a joint line, its masters being the LNW and MS&L, followed by the LMS and LNE until nationalisation at the end of 1947. It carries a heavy suburban traffic and was electrified on the 1500V d.c. system with overhead transmission in 1931. This was superseded by

127

the standard London Midland 25kV a.c. system, to facilitate through running, and at the present time most of the trains on the MSJ&A run through to Alderley Edge or Crewe.

Unlike the main London Road terminal station, the MSJ&A platforms have always carried through traffic. They were treated as a separate station until 1958, when they were merged with the terminal platforms. The first view shows the MSJ&A platform with its tracks equipped for overhead electric working. The brake van of a through westbound train is vanishing from sight at the left of the photograph. In the foreground is the 7.57 from Runcorn, which reached Manchester over the MSJ&A. It consists of LMS compartment stock hauled by 2-4-2 tank locomotive No.50644. This was built by the L&YR at their Horwich Works in 1890, and originally numbered 1047. It became LMS No.10644 and BR No.50644 before withdrawal in 1958. When the photograph was taken it was allocated to Warrington Shed, and bears the Depot Code No.8B on its smokebox door. Typical hand trolleys of the type replaced by 'Brutes' appear in the left foreground. In the background is a BR Mk1 coach in 'plum and spilt milk' livery, forming part of the up 'Mancunian'. The great roofs and windscreens which were constructed over the terminal platforms in 1881 and 1882 dominate the skyline.

Extensive rebuilding took place at London Road as part of the electrification scheme of the early sixties. The MSJ&A platforms were replaced by an island platform further back from the junction with the main line. The new position may be established by reference to the roof spans of the terminal station. There are four of them, and the first view shows parts of the three spans on the south-western side of the station. The second view shows only two of the spans. It will be seen that although the basic structure has not been altered, the glazing of the end windscreens has been modernized. An electric multiple unit train occupies platform 12 on the south-west side of the terminal station. The photograph was taken from the end of the new island platform 13/14. This has new platform buildings and is joined to the main station by the modern footbridge, which is visible in the background. Almost everything in this picture was new in the 1960s, including the overhead electric wiring, the platform lighting, the colour light signalling and the platforms. Perhaps the most traditional object is the milepost showing a distance of $188\frac{3}{4}$ miles from Euston. The juxtaposition of through and terminal platforms is by no means unique – Manchester Victoria, Portsmouth and Southsea and London Bridge are well known examples. However, in most cases there has been a tendency for the through platforms to develop more than terminals, but at Manchester Piccadilly both shared in the investment programme of the 1960s.

198, 199 Werneth Incline, formerly L & YR (SO 904049), on 12 August 1953 and 29 August 1976

The Manchester and Leeds Railway was completed in 1841, with George Stephenson as Engineer, and Thomas Gooch (brother of Daniel) as Resident Engineer. Like the London and Birmingham, the Manchester and Leeds was planned to reach important towns near the line by means of branches, and one of these was to serve Oldham. The branch was planned with a rope-worked incline, and was opened in 1842. It was provided with a double line, but all trains used one track on the incline. They would be assisted up the 1 in 27 gradient, or be checked on their descent, by a balance load ascending or descending the second track. This consisted of wagons which were usually filled with sand or coal when going down, and, by means of a wire rope running round a pulley, assisted another train up the incline. Despite the steepness of the gradient the incline was only about three quarters of a mile long, and, provided trains did not exceed 6 or 7 coaches or 8 or 9 freight wagons, locomotives could rush the bank, and dispense with assistance from the rope, which went out of use in the early 1850s. An alternative route from Manchester, by-passing the incline, was opened in 1880, but passenger trains continued to negotiate the old route until 1958. Even after this an early morning train used the incline, and it was used for Sunday diversions in 1960. Final closure came in 1963.

Both views were taken from the south side of the line, about half way up the incline. In the first view, the foot of the incline is clearly visible under the bridge. The double track consists of conventional bullhead rails in chairs on wooden sleepers. The train is the 16.55 departure from Middleton Junction on the main line, and consists of three LMS compartment coaches hauled by an LMS standard mixed traffic 4-6-0. BR No.44736 was built at Crewe Works in 1949 and withdrawn in 1967. The letters SC under the depot code number on the smokebox door indicate a self cleaning smokebox. With loads of this weight and a run at the bank, it was unusual for a train to fail to reach the top.

The second view records the virtually complete disappearance of Werneth Incline. It was taken from slightly higher up the incline, from a view point a little further to the right. Linkage between the two photographs is provided by the parapet of the road bridge. The cutting to the left of the trees has been filled in, but the bridge and the space underneath it remain. Only the western end, near the foot of the incline, has escaped burial. The steepest incline worked by freight trains was shown in photograph No.177 and may still be seen, but Werneth, once the steepest incline worked by normal passenger trains, has been almost completely obliterated.

200, 201 Line between Lancaster Castle and Lancaster Green Ayre Stations, formerly Midland Railways (SO 473622), on 18 August 1965 and 2 September 1976

The North Western, absorbed by the Midland in 1871, and not to be confused with the LNW, completed their line from Skipton to Lancaster and Morecambe in 1850. In fact, the section from Lancaster to Morecambe was the first part to be opened, in 1848, followed at the end of 1849 by the connection between the North Western's Green Ayre Station and the LNWR's Castle Station. This gave a connection to the West Coast Main Line, but the single-track link was mainly used by local services. In 1904, the Midland opened a new terminal for its Irish steamer services at Heysham, south of Morecambe, and in 1908 it electrified the local service between Heysham, Morecambe and the two Lancaster stations. This was a period when other companies – notably the L&Y and the NE – were introducing local electric services, but the Midland trains were different. Perhaps influenced by a visit of two Midland officials to America, the Lancaster line was electrified on a 6600V 25 cycle a.c. system with overhead wires. The service continued until 1951 when it reverted to steam traction. In 1953, electric services were restored, with LNW stock of 1914 converted to operate on a 6600V 50 cycle a.c. supply. Most of the existing gantries remained in use. The Midland system had not been developed, but this second use of the Lancaster to Morecambe line as a test bed led on to the great electrification projects of the London Midland Region. The volume of traffic was insufficient to support a local electric service, so once the experimental period had passed its days were numbered. In the event, the electric trains were withdrawn in 1966. The spur continued in use for coal traffic to the Lancaster Power Station until 1968.

Both views were taken from a footbridge over the spur line, looking towards the Midland Railway's Green Ayre Station. The spur ran down to the south bank of the River Lune and was joined by the line from Morecambe just west of the station. This crossed from the north bank to the south bank on the curved bridge which appears on the left of the photograph. Despite being summer, it was a cool and rather misty day as the smoking chimneys suggest,

and unfortunately a number of features in the middle distance are not visible. The river bridge with its gantries supporting the live wires appears, as does an end gable of Green Ayre Station on the extreme left. The engine sheds occupy the area to the left of the white building, backed by the industrial area. However, particular interest lies in the original gantries of 1908.

The second view from the same bridge was taken from a position slightly further to the right. A fix is provided by the former railway bridge. The piers were retained but new decking was provided to carry one way traffic on a two lane roadway. Coal traffic running down the spur to the power station crossed the approach to the bridge by a level crossing. A comparable example of the re-use of the piers of a railway bridge to support a new road is to be found over the River Medway at Rochester. Other links between the two views include the roofs in the foreground, and the white building referred to above as a marker for the engine sheds. While it is a truism that every picture tells a story, the explanation of this view would be difficult without some prior knowledge of its history.

202, 203, 204 Woodhead Tunnel, formerly Great Central Railway (SK 113999), on 29 August 1976, about 1906 and on 29 August 1976

The first section of the Sheffield, Ashton-under-Lyne and Manchester Railway was opened in 1841, but it was another four years before the line was opened throughout between Manchester and Sheffield. The main obstacle was the penetration of the Pennines, by means of the great tunnel at Woodhead. Although the construction of a single track bore reduced the amount of work, the length, 3 miles 22 yards, made this the principal engineering work on the line. Excavation was carried out at 12 working faces, 10 of which were at the bottoms of 5 vertical shafts. The number of men employed varied, with an average of around 400, living in primitive conditions on the inhospitable moorland. Work began in 1839, and traffic began passing through the tunnel in December 1845. It increased rapidly and a second bore, parallel to the first, was opened in 1852. The original tunnels ascended at 1 in 201 to a summit near the eastern portal, which exacerbated ventilation problems with steam locomotives. In the 1940s Woodhead was carrying about 80 trains a day, of which the vast majority were coal trains passing from Yorkshire to Lancashire, and the returning empties. In 1936, shortly after the closure of the pioneer electrification for coal traffic between Shildon and Newport Yard near Middlesbrough, the LNER Board approved a scheme for the electrification of the Manchester–Sheffield–Wath lines. This was delayed by the War, but was completed in 1954. Meanwhile the condition of Woodhead Tunnel had deteriorated, and in 1947 the LNER Board decided on the construction of a

new double-track tunnel. Their decision was confirmed by BR and work began in 1949. With electric traction in view, it was decided to move the summit level to a point just over a mile from the eastern portal, thus increasing the gradient faced by eastbound trains from 1 in 207 to 1 in 129. This would facilitate operating if it were decided to permit two trains to be on one line in the tunnel simultaneously. Incidentally, the new tunnel was 44 yards longer than its predecessors but remains the third longest in Britain (it is surpassed by the Severn and Totley tunnels). The accommodation provided at Dunford Bridge Camp was much superior to the shanty towns of the 1840s. Considerable difficulties were encountered, but the new tunnel was officially opened in 1954. Since 1966 the old tunnels have been used to carry electricity.

The first view shows the western portals of the two original, single bore tunnels and the new tunnel, built to take double track and overhead electric wires. Woodhead Station, which was near the western portal, underwent some rebuilding, but was closed in 1964. The platforms remain intact, and the end of one of them adjoins the gantry on the right hand side of the photograph. Colour light signals were provided for the new tunnel and one may be seen to the left of the gantry. The equipment to the left of the chain-link fence marking the railway boundary belongs to the electricity authorities.

The second and third views indicate the change of use of the original tunnel. The line crossed the River Etherow as it approached the portal. The second view is a reproduc-

tion of an F. Moore painting, based on a photograph taken from the far end of the westbound (or down) platform of the old station. It shows the girders, and a central pillar resting on a pier of the bridge over the river. Lower quadrant semaphore signals, typical of the GC, are shown on both tracks, the visibility of the up signal being improved with a white background. Unfortunately the ornate castellated towers above the portals are obscured by steam and smoke. However, a slit designed to fit a mediaeval cross bow is visible on the right. The spacing of the tracks reflects the distance it was necessary to leave between the two borings. The picture includes two express passenger trains. The up or eastbound train is double headed by 4-4-0 locomotives of Pollit's design. The down

train is headed by a GC Atlantic, designed by Robinson. GC No.264 was built by Beyer, Peacock, in 1904. It became LNER No.5264, was re-numbered 2903 in 1946, and was withdrawn in 1949. This evocative view conveys something of the atmosphere of Woodhead in steam days.

The third view was taken from a position slightly nearer the tunnel and further over to the left. The ornamental towers above the portals have been removed, but the tops of the slits are visible on both sides. Wire grills prevent entry by unauthorised persons, and buildings of the electricity authority occupy the foreground. There cannot be many examples of tunnels built to take railway trains which now carry electric cables.

205, 206, 207 Darlington North Road Station, formerly Stockton and Darlington Railway (NZ 289157), on 20 May 1973 and 7 August 1975

The question of whether the Stockton and Darlington Railway of 1825 or the Liverpool and Manchester of 1830 was the first steam railway was discussed in connection with the view of Sankey Viaduct (No.194). Whereas this is a matter for debate, there is no question about the greater development of the S&D before its absorption. The L&M was absorbed by the Grand Junction in 1845, but the S&D continued as an independent company, with important lines reaching out from County Durham into Yorkshire and Westmorland. Formal amalgamation with the North Eastern came in 1863. Because of this, its principal station in Darlington was of some importance. It was the S&D's second Darlington Station, located on the Great North Road about ½ mile north of the town. The 1825 station was sited on the east side of the main road; North Road was opened in the 1840s on the west side. The first Darlington Bank Top Station was opened by the Great North of England Railway in 1841, and in 1887 the construction of a new connecting line placed it on the main S&D route. This, coupled with the demise of the S&D as an independent company, precipitated the decline of the North Road Station. By the early 1970s it retained an hourly service of trains to Bishop Auckland, but had become an unstaffed halt. When preparations for celebrating the 150th anniversary were under way, it was felt that something should be done about the fast-decaying station which had once been the principal establishment of the S&D. Following the initiative of Mr Herbert Wolfe, with co-operation from the local authority, restoration was carried out, and in 1975 North Road achieved the distinction of being both a working railway station and a museum.

The first two views were taken in 1973 before restoration. Basically, the North Road buildings consisted of a large central block, with smaller extensions on both sides. The central block was parallelled by a two span overall roof, one of the few surviving examples of timber construction. This covered a side platform, and an island platform reached by a wooden footbridge. By 1973 only the outer face of the island platform was in use. In fact part of the side platform had been out of use for many years, access to trains being blocked by iron railings along the edge of the platform. (As only a single line existed between the side and island platforms, trains could be reached from the other side of the line.) When the staff were withdrawn the footbridge was closed, and a gangway was constructed across the single track, linking the station entrance and side platform to the trains. Photograph No.205 was taken on the side platform looking to the west, and No.206 from the inner face of the island platform facing in the same direction. Passengers entered through the unstaffed booking hall, gaining access to the platform by the doorway to the left of the spiral staircase. They stepped into an atmosphere of neglect, typified by the only notice, a Pay Train Guide half obliterated by vandals. Access to most of the side platform and also to the footbridge was precluded by gates or temporary wooden barriers. It was possible however to observe the clock, which had lost its hands, and to appreciate the very fine iron spiral staircase which led to a closed door. Illumination was provided by a single gas lamp. The wooden platform had a thin covering of broken glass and other rubbish, but this had accumulated to a greater depth on the disused track between the

platforms. The neglect spread to the footbridge and the overall roof, which were at risk from either fire or decay. It looked as though North Road was doomed.

The third view, taken from the island platform in 1975 and looking to the east, shows the transformation. The ground floor of the building and the area covered by the overall roof have become a museum. Railway passengers have an alternative entrance and skirt the museum premises to reach the trains. The main features, such as the wooden roof and footbridge, have been carefully preserved, and the temporary barricades and gangway have been removed. The most significant changes that have proved necessary are the substitution of electric for gas lighting, and some alterations to the island platform to facilitate inspection of the locomotives on exhibition. In 1975 there were two, that nearest the camera being 0-6-0

No.1275. This was built by Dubs & Co. of Glasgow in 1874 to the design of William Bouch, locomotive engineer of the Stockton and Darlington. It was withdrawn by the LNER in 1925 and appeared in the S&D Centenary Celebrations in that year. After fifty years in the old York Railway Museum it was moved to Darlington in 1975 and appeared in the 150th Anniversary celebrations. Beyond it was No.1463, a 2-4-0 of the Tennant class built at Darlington in 1885. Like No.1275 this took part in the 1925 celebrations and was then preserved in the old York Railway Museum. Another item of rolling stock exhibited but not shown in the photograph was an S&D coach of 1846. North Road is not the only railway station turned into a museum; Monkwearmouth is another example. But at the time of writing, it is the only establishment which combines the functions of museum and railway station.

Largest Railway Crossing in the World, Newcastle-on-Tyne.

208, 209 Newcastle Central, formerly North Eastern Railway (NZ 638250), about 1930 and on 11 April 1964

Both views were taken from the castle, looking down on the eastern end of Newcastle Central Station. This is the busiest station in North East England, and for many years handled about 1200 arrivals and departures daily. It consists of through platforms on the south side, and terminal platforms on the north side at both ends of the station. When it was opened in 1850 Newcastle Central was basically a terminus, with trains on what became part of the East Coast Main Line reversing in the station. This activity was confined to the eastern end. At the beginning of 1851 access from the western end was completed, and trains could reach the station from Carlisle. While the

High Level Bridge provided the crossing of the Tyne for most trains, Newcastle acted as a terminus involving reversal. All was changed in 1906 when the new King Edward Bridge was opened west of the station. Together with new triangular junctions in Gateshead on the south side of the Tyne, this enabled East Coast Main Line trains to call at Newcastle without reversal, and greatly improved traffic flows. Services on the North Tyne lines were electrified in 1904, using the terminal bays at the east end of the station. In 1935 electrification was extended to the South Tyne lines. Post-war road competition led to a decline in traffic to levels at which the renewal of electric equipment could not be justified. The South Tyne lines went over to diesel operation in 1960, followed by the North Tyne in 1967. It is now intended to re-electrify both lines as part of the County of Tyne and Wear's Metro system, and this will result in some abstraction of traffic from Newcastle Central.

The two views show the lines to the north diverging to the right, and those crossing the High Level Bridge into County Durham going off to the left. The first photograph was taken before the electrification of the South Tyne lines, so the live rail is confined to the tracks on the right hand side of the picture. The numerous crossings account for the gaps in the third rail, but as the trains were multiple units this did not present a serious problem. Only two electric trains are visible, at the right hand platform. A steam train of NER coaches with clerestory roofs has passed under the signal gantry and is negotiating a series of crossings on its way to the High Level Bridge (there were 24 diamond crossings). This level crossing between the local and main lines created both operating and maintenance problems. Because of the intensive utilisation, the trackwork was laid out with cast manganese steel in 1924. Although the platforms do project slightly, most of their area was covered by overall roofs. From 1909 the semaphore signals, on the gantry and elsewhere, were operated by an electro-pneumatic system. The small tank locomotive on the right was probably acting as station pilot.

The second view was taken about thirty-four years later. The track layout shows little change, but signalling and motive power have both been altered. The semaphore signals have been replaced by colour lights. The steam station pilot has been replaced by the diesel attached to the Royal Mail coaches alongside the freight train. Instead of a local passenger train on the crossing, the second view shows a diesel hauled freight train making for the North. The locomotive is Class 40 No.D399 (now 40199). This was built by English Electric and Vulcan Foundry in 1962. Still unchanged when the photograph was taken were the North Tyneside multiple unit electrics, and two are shown at the same platform (one is almost concealed by the station roof). A striking difference is the removal of a considerable area of roofing on the left, possibly as a result of enemy action. But giving due weight to these points, the east end of Newcastle Central is not an example of extreme change in the railway scene.

8 Wales

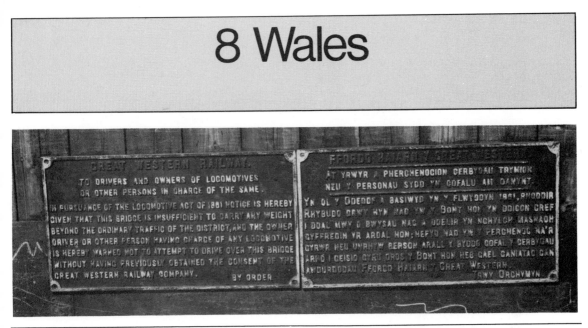

210 Blaenau Festiniog, overbridge on former GWR (SH 702458) on 21 April 1965

In contrast to Scotland, much of Wales was served by English railway companies, in particular the LNWR and the GWR. One of the reasons for this was the use of Wales as a land bridge for the two main routes to Ireland. The English companies, however, did make some adaptations, such as the provision of notices in Welsh in Welsh-speaking parts of the Principality. In 1882 the Great Western reached the slate-producing town of Festiniog and the following year widened an existing narrow-gauge line in order to extend to Blaenau Festiniog. The pair of cast iron notices illustrated were placed on an overbridge in Blaenau, and demonstrate adjustment to Wales.

211, 212 Morfa Mawddach, formerly Cambrian Railways (SH 628142), on 15 August 1966 and 17 July 1975

The Cambrian Coast line of BR began as the Aberystwyth and Welsh Coast Railway, absorbed by the Cambrian Railways in 1865. Lack of money combined with engineering difficulties led to opening in sections. The main line from Aberystwyth to Pwllheli was planned to cross two estuaries – the Dovey near Aberdovey and the Mawddach near Barmouth. In the event, the bridge across the estuary of the Dovey was never built and trains between Aberystwyth and Aberdovey have to make a long detour inland. Traffic from England was fed onto the coast line from the Cambrian main line at Machynlleth and from the Great Western at Dolgellau. The first sections of the coast line were opened in 1863 and it was completed, with the bridge across the Mawddach and the diversion around the Dovey, in 1867. Traffic was fed on to it via Machynlleth at once but it was not until 1869 that connection was made with the GWR at Dolgellau. The line ran through Penmaenpool to a triangular junction with the coast line near the southern end of the great bridge over the Mawddach. GW trains ran through to Barmouth, but usually with Cambrian locomotives beyond Dolgellau. A station was opened at the northern end of the triangular junction. Single lines radiated in all three directions, but two sides of the triangle, the NW and the NE, were provided with double track and side platforms. (The third side of the triangle had single track and no platforms.) In 1960, Barmouth Junction, for want of a nearby settlement with a name to offer, became Morfa Mawddach. It lost its goods depot in 1963, and, in December 1964, its connection to Dolgellau. (Official closure in January 1965 was anticipated by floods breaking the line.) At this time it was the berthing place for two camping coaches, but they were withdrawn, together with the station staff, in 1968. In turn the signals, the tracks (except for one running line) and all the buildings disappeared. Barmouth Junction has become an unstaffed halt.

Both views were taken from the north end of the station looking south. Although the left hand line, leading to Dolgellau, had been closed in the previous year, the only visible impact of the closure in the first view is the removal of the arms of the bracketed starting signal. The 20 mph speed restriction sign, with an arrow indicating its applicability to the Dolgellau direction, remains in position, together with the tracks and associated signal wires and point rodding. The signal box is Cambrian but the signals are Great Western. The station buildings, constructed in the vee between the converging routes, are notable for their unusual plan, which is followed on three sides by a canopy supported on iron columns. As its original name of Barmouth Junction implies, the station was mainly designed for passengers changing between the coastal and inland lines, but it did have road access by means of a level crossing over the rarely used third side of the triangle.

The second view shows the impact of rationalisation. Only one track remains, and one platform face out of the four is still in use. All the buildings have been demolished, except for the iron shed used by permanent way staff. The only visible station facilities are a lamp and a nameboard. Probably this paucity reflects the traffic of the station, deprived of its junction status. Platforms and telegraph poles provide a link between past and present at Morfa Mawddach.

213, 214 Machynlleth, formerly Cambrian Railways (SH 745014), on 20 August 1966 and 6 April 1973

Reference has already been made to the coast line joining the main line to England at Machynlleth. The main line was completed by four companies in a number of sections, finally reaching Whitchurch in 1864. The companies amalgamated to form the Cambrian Railways in 1864, and as mentioned above, the Cambrian absorbed the coastal railway in 1865. Even after years of amalgamation, Machynlleth always appeared a point of division between the inland and coastal lines of the Cambrian.

Both views were taken from trains standing in the up platform and looking east, with the line into England curving away beyond the engine shed. The first view was taken from the window of a BR Mk1 coach in maroon livery, at the head of a through train to Paddington. All four locomotives in the photograph are standard BR 4-6-0s of the 75XXX class. A pilot locomotive is backing onto the train for the climb through the hills and will be detached at Welshpool. Both locomotives seem to have a good head of steam for the difficult road ahead. Machynlleth M.P.D. was built in two stages, the older being the section with the roof and prominent ventilators and the newer being roofless. It closed as a steam shed in December 1966. The curved bar to the right of the shed is part of a loading gauge. As would be expected, Macnynlleth was a passing place on the single track Cambrian, and with a goods yard and engine sheds on opposite sides of the line, had a fairly complex layout.

The second view was taken from the front of a diesel multiple unit train, through both the windscreen and the glass in the bulkhead separating the driver's cab from the passenger accommodation. By this time through trains to Paddington were a thing of the past and the train was terminating at Shrewsbury. Links between the two views are provided by the foot level crossing, made of old sleepers, and the engine shed. By the time of the second photograph this was re-roofed and in use as a diesel depot. The modern BR signal box was obscured in the first view but appears in the second, together with the down home signal and a warning to passengers against using the level crossings. There has been some simplification of layout, and the up starting signal, bracketed with an arm for a loop line in the earlier photograph, is on a plain post. While the detailed changes are significant, perhaps the most striking contrast is in the quiet of the later view against the more dramatic atmosphere of the days of steam.

215, 216 Three Cocks Station, formerly Cambrian Railways (SO 176373), on 11 September 1951 and 14 August 1970

Three Cocks Station was sited at the physical junction of the lines from Llanidloes and from Hereford to Talyllyn Junction for Brecon. There was no settlement in the immediate vicinity, so the station took its name from a nearby hostelry. The general arrangement was the same as that at Morfa Mawddach, with double track and side platforms on each of the diverging lines. The first view was taken from the Hay and Hereford side, looking south towards the physical junction. Both the signal cabin and the starting signal for the Mid-Wales line from Llanidloes belong to the Cambrian. On the other hand the buildings, with the notice proclaiming 'Refreshment Rooms', are typical of the Mid-Wales. This also applies to the wooden lamp posts with their oil lamps and the lack of any canopy over the platform. The stone-faced platforms with blue brick copings were never raised to standard height, and the steps, appearing in the foreground, were available to

help the less agile to mount or dismount from trains. The two station nameboards are complementary, that on the Hereford platform inviting change for a list of places on the Mid-Wales line, and that on the Mid-Wales line referring to places on the Hereford line.

The second view was taken after the removal of the tracks and the filling in of the space between the platforms. The main station building has become the Three Cocks Depot of the Calor Gas Group, with very few alterations. Not only the sash windows but also decorative features, such as the barge-boards on the gables, and the ornate ridge tiles, appear in both photographs. However, without prior knowledge, there is little to indicate that this was once a railway station, a remark probably applicable to many stations in rural Wales. Three Cocks may now vibrate with the arrival and departure of motor cars, but its former railway function belongs to the past.

217, 218 Sudbrook Pumping Station, formerly GWR (ST 506874), on 17 March 1957 and 16 July 1976

The Severn Tunnel is the longest in Britain. Of its $4\frac{1}{2}$ miles, about half is under the River Severn, three eighths under Monmouthshire and one eighth under Gloucestershire. It was authorised in 1872, and work commenced in the following year. The greatest setbacks were the floodings of 1879 and 1883. The tunnel was finally opened in 1886, giving greatly improved access to South Wales, especially from Bristol and the West Country. A line just under a mile in length was constructed from the South Wales main line at Caldicot Pill, over the centre line of the tunnel to a shaft on the Monmouthshire side at Sudbrook. This was in position by 1879 and is still intact. Its initial function was to bring in supplies, including coal for working the pumps, and it continued to bring in coal until the pumping station was electrified.

The first view shows the line to Sudbrook and the pumping station in steam days. Housing was constructed on either side of the line, but stone walls separated the railway from the roads which flanked it. Unconventional metal gates operated by train crews protected the level crossing. The large water tank adjoined the engine house. Between 23 and 30 million gallons a day could be pumped from the tunnel and there were 8 pumping engines at Sudbrook. All were built by Harveys of Hayle in Cornwall. Six were Cornish-type beam engines and two were Bull

engines. There was also a ventilating fan, 40 feet in diameter and 12 feet wide, but this is not visible on the photograph. The number of chimneys reflect the amount of steam raised to drive the machinery which drained and ventilated the tunnel. An unusual feature on the day on which this photograph was taken was the presence of the District Engineer's Inspection Saloon from Newport, attached to the tank engine in the middle distance.

The first view was taken on a cold and damp day in winter, and the second on a very hot summer's day. There are minor changes in the foreground in the second view. The warning notice by the crossing has been knocked off its post, perhaps in the same accident that demolished a length of the wall. There is a new warning notice and a new length of chain link fencing with concrete posts. The track and crossing gates seem unaltered. Of the buildings on either side of the views, the school on the extreme left shows little change, but the building on the right has been renovated and opened as a club. The water tank and pump house remain, although the latter now contains electric pumps which can hardly use its full height. All four chimneys have been demolished. The electrification at Sudbrook greatly reduced the employment available. However, a paper works has been opened at the other end of this very unusual Victorian new village, and the condition of the houses suggests a degree of prosperity.

219, 220 Penrhyn Point, Fairbourne Railway (SH 617150), about 1912 and on 30 July 1972

Photos 160 to 162 illustrated the way in which a standard gauge branch line had been transformed into a narrow gauge electric railway, mainly for pleasure rides. The Fairbourne Railway has an even more unusual history. In the 1890s, following the opening of the coastal section of the Cambrian Railways, building development sprouted at various places. Usually these adjoined old established ports, such as Pwllheli or Barmouth, but at Fairbourne houses were constructed on flat land behind the storm beach of Ro Wen. For many years a road had followed the spit with its sand dunes, which had been built up by beach drift across the Mawddach estuary. From its extremity at Penrhyn Point a ferry crossed to Barmouth. The developer of Fairbourne, Mr McDougall of Self Raising Flour fame, constructed a 2 foot gauge horse tramway about 2 miles long; it went from a brickworks, alongside the Cambrian main line, passing through his housing estate and running out along a spit to the Barmouth Ferry. It carried supplies for the estate, and also passengers. An alternative route to Barmouth was provided from 1899, when the Cambrian built a station at Fairbourne. The horse tramway and ferry remained an attraction to summer visitors, but its role as a means of transport was diminished. In 1916 Narrow Gauge Railways Ltd, who were already operating a number of 15 inch gauge lines, regauged the Fairbourne, and introduced a steam locomotive and four passenger cars. Subsequently, there have been changes of ownership, and summers without trains (the longest gap was between 1939 and 1947). Since the

Second World War additional locomotives, both steam and diesel, have been added to stock, and a new station has been built at Fairbourne. The line depends mainly on pleasure traffic and has benefitted from the corporate sales policy of the Welsh narrow gauge railways.

Both views were taken at the extremity of the spit looking across to Barmouth. There is a considerable overlap between the two views, but the horse tramway view is inclined more to the left (the west), and the second view more to the right. The first view shows the 2 foot gauge track, running across the sands. The horse is pulling one of the two passenger cars, which were basically flat platforms with three back-to-back seats. Even in summer there must have been times when the passengers would have appreciated rather more protection from the elements.

The second view shows a typical train of the post-war period on 15 inch gauge track. A low platform, with a seat, a nameboard and rail-borne refreshment vehicle have been provided. The ferry leaves from the beach on the left. The well-patronised train consists mainly of open stock but does include one of the closed cars. There is a run-round loop but no turntable at the Ferry station, and so the locomotive, 'Siân', is ready to return to Fairbourne running tender first. 'Siân' is a 2-4-2, built by G & S Ltd to a special design by E.W. Twining and delivered to Fairbourne in 1963. In a sense, the Fairbourne is one of the few narrow gauge lines which have run boat trains.

221, 222 Near Mumbles Pier, formerly Swansea and Mumbles Railway (SS 625877), about 1910 and on 5 August 1958

A conventional railway and a street tramway are sufficiently distinctive, although they both use wheels on rails. Between the two extremes, forms of transport such as the American inter-urbans or the Belgian vicinals occupy an intermediate position. In Britain, lines such as that between Blackpool and Fleetwood carried both passengers and freight, and had considerable lengths of track on their own right of way. They were rare, and although the Blackpool and Fleetwood remains open for passengers only, the Swansea and Mumbles closed at the beginning of 1960. The line from Swansea to the seaside village of Oystermouth, with a branch to a colliery, was

authorised in 1804. It was laid with plate rails, and a passenger service – perhaps the first regular public service in the world over rails – was introduced in 1807. However, a turnpike road was constructed from Swansea to Oystermouth in about 1826, and for a period the passenger service was by road rather than by rail. Edge rails were substituted for plate rails in 1855 and passenger traffic, conveyed by double deck coaches, was resumed on the railway in 1860. However, the Oystermouth Railway ran into financial difficulties and from 1877 its track was used by the Swansea Improvements and Tramway Company. Their particular contribution was the introduction of steam traction. There followed a phase of difficult and complicated relations between the railway and tramways companies, with a period during which the railway company was using steam locomotives while the tramway company had reverted to horse traction. The Oystermouth Railway was reconstituted as the Swansea & Mumbles Railway Ltd, and was associated with the Mumbles Railway and Pier Company. The latter extended the line from Oystermouth to Mumbles head, opening the railway to Southend in 1893 and to Mumbles and the pier in 1898. The complexities were resolved in 1899 when the Swansea Improvement and Tramway Company leased the two railway companies for 999 years. In 1929, the tramway company was considering the abandonment of its tram routes, and the unexpired portion of the lease was transferred to the bus company which was taking over the services – namely the South Wales Transport Co. This led to the unusual situation of a railway, carrying passenger and goods traffic, being operated by a bus company. The Swansea and Mumbles was electrified in 1929. The steam locomotives and the associated double deck cars were disposed of, passenger working being taken over by electrically-powered double deck cars, and freight (mostly coal and coke) by a petrol locomotive which was joined by a diesel in 1936. Traffic reached a peak of about 5 million in 1945, and even in 1953 the line carried 3,150,000 passengers. However, when the equipment was near the end of its working life, it was decided that the service could be more economically provided by buses. The end section, between Southend and Mumbles Pier, was closed in November 1959 and the rest of the line in January 1960.

Photos 221 and 222 were taken on the extension, at the approach to the Mumbles Pier terminus. No.221 was taken on a holiday before the First World War, when the Mumbles had attracted large numbers of visitors. About 12 very well loaded cars appear on the photograph, but as trains sometimes consisted of up to twenty cars, much of the train is not shown. (Incidentally, about 1800 passengers were carried at busy times on one train, hauled by one locomotive, in conditions approaching those associated with Indian railways.) The first class and composite cars ran on bogies; second class were four wheelers. All were double deckers with open tops, but the first class upper decks had garden type seats and the second class had knifeboard benches. They were provided with railway type buffers and ordinary screw couplings. As the trains were not fitted with continuous brakes, it is not surprising that average speeds were about 7 or 8 mph. The car in the foreground is of the toast-rack type. Unfortunately the locomotive is only indicated by a puff of steam, but the Swansea and Mumbles used tank locomotives with either the 0-4-0 or 0-6-0 wheel arrangement. Platforms were not provided at the stations, as indicated by the footboards on the cars. Moreover, as boarding was always on the landward side, entrances were confined to one side of the cars.

The second view was taken in roughly the same place, under rather quieter traffic conditions nearly fifty years later. There would be little difference in the standard gauge flat-bottomed track, spiked to wooden sleepers. However, the track is on the site of the engine run round loop, on the seaward side of the train in the first view. The overhead wires, supported by brackets attached to side poles carried 650V dc. Current was returned through the running rails in the normal way. The double wiring was necessitated by the heavy demand for current, especially when the cars were operating in pairs. The substation, at Black Pill, took current at 6.6kV ac which was converted to 650V dc by rotary converters. The 'train' approaching consists of 2 of the standard electric cars, running as a multiple unit.

223, 224 Black Pill, formerly Swansea and Mumbles Railway (SS 619907), about 1958 and on 8 September 1971

The two views at Black Pill are taken from approximately the same position, looking towards Swansea. No.223 shows running track and electric wiring similar to that described for No.222. However, an additional feature is the two rails in the middle of the track, added to increase the cross-section of rail available for return current. It will be noted that the Swansea and Mumbles was operated basically as a single track line with passing places. When the line was electrified, 11 new cars of unusually high capacity were ordered, and the total stock was increased to 13 in the following year. Built by Brush, and seating 106 passengers, 48 in the lower saloon and 58 on the top deck, they were the largest tramcars in Britain. They could be driven from either end, singly or in pairs. Both the motors and the air brakes were supplied by British Thomson-Houston of Rugby. Current collection was by pantographs. Like the steam-hauled cars which they replaced, they had both front and rear entrances on the landward side. (This did of course, make it necessary to provide space between the tracks for passengers at stations where the loading point was on a passing loop, as at Southend.) There were no signals in steam days, the schedule of 30 minutes for $5\frac{1}{2}$ miles permitting cautious running. However, with electrification the journey time

was reduced to 19 minutes, and specially designed colour light signals were introduced to control the working over the single track sections. One of these is visible in the photograph. There were also mechanical point locks and electrical point detectors. To the right of the side pole, a semaphore signal is visible on the former LNWR line from Gowerton to Swansea, closed to all traffic in 1965.

The second photograph shows the same site in 1971, with the colonnade on the left and the former LNW railway embankment linking the two views. It cannot be claimed that they were taken on the line opened in 1806, as in 1900 a new alignment was adopted from a point on the Swansea side of Black Pill to Oystermouth. This removed the line from the side of a narrow road which, beyond Black Pill, was increasingly built up.

It is of interest to compare the very different stories of two roadside railways, the Swansea and Mumbles and the Wisbech and Upwell. In the latter case, passenger traffic faded rapidly and freight sustained the line. In the former, passenger traffic, encouraged by electrification, remained heavy up to the day of closure. It was one of the few lines on which horses, steam and electricity had all provided power – and if the freight traffic be included, also the internal combustion engine. In 1860, it regained traffic previously lost to the parallel road, but this is not likely to happen again.

9 Scotland

225 Prestonpans Station, formerly North British Railway (NT 393738), on 27 April 1966

The main line of the North British Railway between Edinburgh and the border at Berwick was opened in 1846. Initially there were gaps in what was to become the East Coast main line; the Royal Border Bridge at Berwick was not finished until 1850. Prestonpans was one of the original stations, although it was named Tranent until 1858. (In fact a short mineral branch was opened to serve the coal pits at Tranent, but this did not carry passengers.) In 1968 Prestonpans was closed to freight traffic, but it retains its passenger service.

Photograph No.225 was taken from the footbridge looking to Berwick. In the centre is an iron trespass warning notice, mounted on a rail, and establishing the owners of the station as the 'North British Railway'. Prestonpans was still open for goods traffic, and the interior of a typical goods shed, with its wooden platform, is shown. Traditional signalling was in use, and although no signals are visible, the lower part of a typical NB signal cabin may be seen at the end of the down platform. The track was of the standard BR flat-bottomed type, later to be replaced by continuous welded rail. The end of a diesel multiple-unit train may be seen on the down line. Although this view was taken in the middle of what was, for the railways, the painful sixties, it shows a scene which as far as the station is concerned could have been taken in the later days of the North British.

226 The entrance to St Boswells Station, formerly North British Railway (NT 577316), on 5 September 1959

The North British provided the Scottish section of the East Coast main line. In addition, by way of their Waverley route from Carlisle to Edinburgh, they competed with the Caledonian for Edinburgh traffic using the West Coast main line. The Waverley route was named because of the association of the district it served with the novels of Sir Walter Scott. It was opened in two sections, from Edinburgh via Galashiels and St Boswells, to Hawick in 1849 and between Hawick and Carlisle in 1862. South of St Boswells the branch to Kelso was opened in 1851, and to the north the Berwickshire Railway to Reston on the East Coast main line was opened in 1865. The importance of St Boswells as a junction declined in stages. First of all part of the Berwickshire Railway was closed in 1948, following severe flood damage. The Kelso line was closed to passengers in 1964 and to all traffic in 1968. Finally, in 1969, the Waverley route was closed and St Boswells lost its trains after 120 years.

The photograph shows the solid construction of a North

British station, as built in 1904. It is difficult to imagine that the number of passengers necessitated the division of those ascending and those descending the staircase, but this was certainly provided for, with Way Out and Way In described in stone. (Incidentally, right hand running was prescribed.) There is an assumption of responsibility, both in the prominent statement of ownership by the letters NBR and in the marking of the date for the information of future generations. The use of stone is notable; in fact, apart from a wooden gate and metal pipes, railings and a column, everything is made of stone. The Morris light van and the dress of the group around it have already acquired a period flavour. Just as in 1904 the NBR would have found it difficult to accept that in 20 years' time their company would have been absorbed into the LNER, so the members of the group would not have believed that within 10 years their station, on a main line between England and Scotland, would be closed.

---

227 Arisaig, formerly North British Railway (NM 664867), on 26 July 1954

The lowland railways of Scotland differ slightly in atmosphere from those of England, mainly because they were built by Scottish companies. But the railways of the Highlands are even more distinctive, both in character and in the setting in which they operate. Their construction dates tend to be later. For instance, the original West Highland was opened from Craigendoran on the Clyde to

Fort William in 1894, and the extension to the small port of Mallaig in 1901. The West Highland was operated by the North British, who in 1908, absorbed the independent company. However, its distinctive stations continued to remind passengers that the West Highland was built by a separate company. Needless to say, traffic was sparse, but the difficulties of road operation increased the importance

147

of the railway to the community and the main line to Fort William and Mallaig remains open.

There were no large settlements which demanded stations, and in most cases stations were located at convenient points at which freight and passengers from quite wide areas could join the railway. However, Arisaig was one of the larger villages which, when its station was opened, was a regular calling place for the steamers from Glasgow to the Isle of Skye. Like most of the stations on the West Highland it was a passing place, although on the Mallaig extension side platforms rather than island platforms were provided. This is shown in photograph No.227, which was taken from the down platform. The signal is one of the lower quadrant type with lattice posts supplied for the opening of the line by Mackenzie and Holland. (The arm was replaced by an upper quadrant in January 1955.) The point rodding to the facing points at the entrance to the loop and the up home signal are visible. The locomotive is K4 class No.61998, designed for the LNER to work on the West Highland. It was built at Darlington Works in 1938 and withdrawn in 1961. The West Highland has been dieselised for some years, and most of the intermediate stations have lost their freight facilities. The depot at Arisaig was closed in 1965. But nearly all the passenger stations remain open and the West Highland has changed less in its character than most of the British railways.

228, 229 Cowlairs Incline, formerly North British Railway (NS 598672), about 1900 and on 1 August 1953

The Edinburgh and Glasgow Railway was opened in 1842. Joining the two principal cities of Scotland it had a number of points in common with the London and Birmingham Railway. One of these was the possession of a well-graded line with heavy-engineering works but, owing to the presence of a canal in each case, one terminal was reached by a steeply-graded rope worked incline. In the case of the L&B this was the Camden Incline necessitated by the Regents Canal, and for the E&G Cowlairs Incline was imposed in order to pass under the Port Dundas extension of the Forth and Clyde Canal. Cowlairs incline consisted of over a mile at 1 in 41 and 1 in 43. Locomotives were attached to their trains at Queen Street, but were assisted by a cable worked from a stationary engine until 1909. Braking was at least as much of a problem as traction before the advent of continuous brakes, and special braking trucks were provided (the NBR used the spelling 'Break'). After 1909 ascending trains were assisted with banking engines, but since the advent of dieselisation power to weight ratios are usually suf-

ficiently favourable to enable trains to go up the incline without assistance.

The first photograph was taken about the turn of the century from the east side of the line. It shows the two tracks leading to Queen Street, and a third track at a higher level which diverged to serve the goods yards at Pinkston and Craighall. The train has covered about two-thirds of the incline, and the fireman of the leading engine is leaving the cab before making his way along the footplate to slip the cable. This was done without stopping the train. The special connection to carry out this operation, including the length of chain on the end of the steel cable and the mechanism above the buffer beam, appear in the photograph. The steel cable resting in its sheaves is also visible on the other track. The Edinburgh express consists mostly of compartment coaches, with a

van and a guard's van at the head of the train. Both locomotives are 4-4-0s of Holmes design with 7 foot driving wheels, with No.598 leading. This was built at Cowlairs Works in 1888 and was withdrawn as LNER No.9598 in 1930.

The second photograph was taken from almost the same place. The power station is an addition to the scene, but the third line to the goods depots gives a fix. In this case the train consists of ex-LNER coaches, one of which is in BR 'plum and spilt milk' livery. The locomotive is of the Scottish Director class, a GC design modified for operating in Scotland. The LNER classification was D11/2. No.62687 was built by Armstrong, Whitworth in 1924 as No.6394 and withdrawn in 1961. Comparison of the two express trains gives a striking impression of the change in locomotives and coaches in fifty years.

230, 231 Benderloch Station, formerly caledonian Railway (NM 903382), on 19 April 1952 and 2 September 1968

Penetration to the west of the Highlands came comparatively late in the railway history of Scotland. The Callander and Oban Railway was authorised in 1865, but such were the constructional and financial problems that Oban was not reached until 1880. Perhaps stimulated by developments associated with the rival North British company, powers were obtained in 1897 to build a railway from

Connel Ferry, on the Oban line, following the coast to Ballachulish for much of its length. However, major bridges were required at Connel Ferry and at Creagan. The line, $27\frac{3}{4}$ miles in length, was opened in 1903.

The second station, opened $2\frac{3}{4}$ miles from Connel, served a district rather than a particular settlement, and took the district name of Benderloch. It had a passing loop

and was signalled from a typical Caledonian signal cabin. The station buildings were distinctive in style, incorporating the usual offices and the station master's house. All these features appear in photograph No.230 taken from a train leaving the down platform. Rain shines on the coping stone of the up platform as the passengers make their way to the exit. A wagon and a van are visible in the goods yard at the back of the platform. This was closed in 1965, and the last passenger train ran in 1966.

The second view, like the first, was taken in the rain, but from the edge of a platform rather than a train. The most striking changes, apart from the removal of the track and the signals, are the disappearance of the signal box and of part of the canopy. Caravans occupy both the track-bed and part of the down platform. In the first photograph the car parked by the station was probably meeting the train, but in the second the cars must have belonged to the people in the caravans. It is most unlikely that the Ballachulish line ever earned its keep, but it is also true that it is still missed in Benderloch.

232, 233, 234 Inverness Station, formerly Highland Railway (NH 668455), on 13 September 1972

Even now Inverness has only about 35,000 inhabitants but, because it has for long been regarded as the capital of the Highlands, it is not surprising that it was served by a local railway before it was connected to the national network. The Inverness and Nairn was opened in 1855, and was regarded as a first step towards Aberdeen and the Lowlands. The Great North of Scotland was planned to link Aberdeen and Inverness but only got as far as Keith. The gap between Nairn and Keith via Forres and Elgin was closed by the Inverness and Aberdeen Junction Railway, opened in 1858. However, the route to the Lowlands via Aberdeen was very circuitous, and in 1863 the Inverness and Perth Junction completed the route from Forres to Perth. The I&AJ and the I&PJ amalgamated to form the Highland Railway in 1865. Beyond Inverness, the first section of the Inverness & Ross-shire had been opened as far as Dingwall in 1862. The existing station at Inverness was retained, but consisted of separate terminal platforms for trains for the South and trains for the North. The lines to the Far North were extended beyond Dingwall and in 1898 the new cut-off line via Carr Bridge gave Inverness an improved connection to the Lowlands.

The most noteworthy engineering work on the Inverness and Aberdeen Junction was the bridge over the River Spey at Orton. This was regarded with such pride as to move the Board to have special iron plates cast, one commemorating the Bridge and a second commemorating themselves. Probably when the bridge was rebuilt in 1906 these were moved to the Highland's principal station, where people could see them. They still do, as photos 232 to 234 show. As mentioned above, Inverness Station consists of two parts, platforms 1 to 4 serving the southbound trains and platforms 5 to 7 for the Far North. The plates were strategically placed on opposite sides of a wall between the two sections. No.232 shows the setting of the plate commemorating the opening of the bridge. Mounted on the same wall is a bell; these are of course more frequently associated with churches, schools and early factories, but hand or mounted bells were in use at many stations to signal departures, in some cases until 1939. Part of the concourse is shown, covered by its overall roof, and also the tracks for platforms 4 and 5 with a siding in between. No.Sc4246 was an Open Second Class coach of the BR Mk1 design introduced in 1951.

No.233 is a close view of the bridge plate. The coat of arms of the Inverness and Aberdeen Junction and of some of the Directors are displayed in a magnificent casting. The plates were originally placed on arches over the track on the bridge, and in that position must have had few readers. A clear distinction was made between those who did the work, and the Board who were responsible for it, each being recorded on separate plates. The original bridge was described by Joseph Mitchell at the British Association Meeting in Dundee in 1867. It consisted of a box girder of 230 feet with six side-arches of masonry. As recorded on the plate, the contractors for the masonry were David Mitchell and Chas. Brand, Montrose, and for the ironwork Messrs Fairbairn and Sons, Manchester. The engineer was Joseph Mitchell, FRSE, Inverness.

No.234 shows the plate, now mounted on the opposite side of the wall. The list of directors and other promoters is headed by Alex Matheson Esq., of Ardross, MP, and Chairman. With two exceptions, all the names are Scottish, and the two exceptions both had strong links with the Highlands. In a period of change, such features as the plates from the original bridge over the River Spey are at risk, and it is fortunate that when the iron span was replaced in 1906, they were not only preserved but were placed where many more people could see them.

151

235, 236 Original station at Forres, Inverness and Aberdeen Junction Railway (NJ 032591), on 16 June 1962 and 11 September 1972

As mentioned, the Inverness and Aberdeen Junction closed the gap between Nairn and Keith via Forres and Elgin in 1858. When the Inverness and Perth Junction was constructed, one of the reasons for selecting Forres as the point of junction was its intermediate position between Inverness and Keith. It was decided to give improved access to Perth and the lowlands from both directions, so a triangular junction was decided upon. The I&PJ opened a new station with platforms on all three sides of the triangle to the south west of the original I&AJ station. Presumably railway politics were involved; otherwise it is not clear why the northern side of the triangle should not have consisted of a section of the I&AJ line to the west of their original station. In any case in 1865, two years after the opening of the new line to Perth and the new Forres Station, the companies amalgamated to form the Highland Railway. The length of the original line which had been by-passed by the opening of the I&PJ station and the new lines was retained for goods traffic, and the old station was used as the station master's residence.

The first view shows the 1858 station with the original I&AJ line to the left. The new line of 1863 comes in from behind the station on the right, the site of the junction being to the left of the disused telegraph pole. Evidently the original route was not regarded as a normal running line,

as protection for the junction is limited to catch points and a ground signal. For running in the opposite direction from the main line, a signal arm for the old route is located on a bracket half way up the post visible in front of the tree on the left. The 1858 building is characteristic of its period, with a hint of classicism in the columns supporting the canopy and in a gable which approaches the proportions of a pediment. Unfortunately by 1962 the building was uninhabited, a residence in a goods yard presumably lacking appeal. The garden was overgrown and the platform obscured by vegetation.

The second view shows the site ten years later, with the track acting as a link between the two photographs. The angle is not the same, the first view being to the ENE and the second to the NNE. The track which served the works on the left has been cut back to the limit of railway property and provided with a buffer stop. A crossover has been inserted linking it to the through line. The ground signal has been replaced by a normal upper quadrant signal mounted on a metal post, but the catch points have been retained. A second additional signal is visible to the right, located on the new main line, but the post with the bracketed arm remains unchanged. The demolition of the old station is entirely in accordance with trends in the changing railway scene, but the addition of signals is rather unusual.

The Morayshire Railway was originally a local undertaking. In 1846 it planned to link the county town of Elgin to its port of Lossiemouth. The Great North of Scotland in the same year was authorised to build its line from Aberdeen to Inverness. The Morayshire planned to use about 10 miles of the GNS between Elgin and Orton, and from there build its own line to Rothes and Dandaleith for Craigellachie. At this stage the GNS got no further than Keith, and the Morayshire confined itself to opening its Elgin to Lossiemouth line in 1852. However, when the Inverness and Aberdeen Junction obtained powers to fill the gap between Nairn and Keith, the Morayshire revived its plans, using the I&AJ between Elgin and Orton. The line from Orton to Rothes and Dandaleith was opened in 1858. However, relations with the I&AJ proved difficult, and so in 1862 the Morayshire opened its own line between Elgin and Rothes. To the south the Strathspey Railway and the Keith and Dufftown were planned together to link the railhead of the GNS at Keith to Granton-on-Spey (subsequently extended to a junction with the Inverness and Perth Junction at Boat of Garten). The Morayshire obtained powers to extend its line from Dandaleith across the Spey to join the Strathspey in a new Craigellachie Station. This was opened in 1863. The GNS took over the working of the Morayshire and the other two companies, and in 1866 closed the connection between Rothes and what had become the Highland Railway, at Orton. It now had its own route between Keith and Elgin. The passenger service between Craigellachie and Boat of Garten was withdrawn in 1965, although freight trains ran as far as Aberlour until 1971. The route from Keith to Elgin via Craigellachie was closed to passengers in 1968. However, until 1971 as mentioned, freight trains ran from Keith via Craigellachie as far as Aberlour via the Speyside line.

The independent Morayshire company's line to Rothes diverged from the Lossiemouth line on the outskirts of Elgin and curved round to the south, crossing over the I&AJ line to the east of the town. Between the junction and the underbridge was Pinefield Level Crossing. This was equipped with the trespass notice illustrated. Iron castings had been fairly standard, but the GNS notice consisted of an enamelled plate of the type developed for advertisement purposes. This probably reflected the late date of 1909 and may also owe something to the Great North of Scotland's necessary tendency to thrift.

153

238, 239 Craigellachie Station, formerly Great North of Scotland Railway (NJ 293452), on 11 April 1946 and 10 September 1972

As mentioned above, the first Craigellachie Station was on the north bank of the Spey at Dandaleith. Perhaps this was the reason for the new station being called Strathspey Junction until 1864. The physical junction was at the south end of the station, the Strathspey line curving sharply away to the west (on the left of the first photograph) to avoid a crossing of the Spey. The viaduct carrying the Elgin line over the river is visible under the span of the road bridge. The first view was taken looking to the north from platform 1, described by the plate on the bridge as being 'For Keith, Aberdeen, Dundee and the South'. Platform 2 has a corresponding plate 'For Elgin, Lossiemouth, Inverness and the North'. Platforms 3 and 4, serving the Strathspey line, were on the opposite side of the station approach. Tall lattice posts, characteristic of the Scottish companies, are visible at the north end of the station. Oil lamps are provided, one at the left hand side of the bridge being raised or lowered by a windlass. Although the signals are on, the gathering of passengers

suggests that a train was due from Elgin. On the opposite platform, a postman waits talking to the man who is supported by a trolley, and the postman's Morris van is at the foot of the station approach. The modest waiting room and the austere footbridge, lacking both sides and roof, were fairly typical of the GNS.

The second view was taken from about the same position, four years after the withdrawal of passenger services. Two structures visible in the first view, the waiting room and the lamp room by the wing of the road bridge, have both been removed. The footbridge and the viaduct have also gone. However, the stone-faced platforms and the station approach road provide links between the two photographs. While the railway has gone, road traffic has been provided with a stronger bridge, a ferro-concrete span having replaced metal. The demand for land in Craigellachie may be insufficient to lead to the rapid removal of what is left of the station, but it no longer plays any part in the lives of the local people.

10 Miscellanea

240 Track at St Keyne, Liskeard and Looe Railway (SX 252609), about 1905

A canal was opened from Liskeard to the estuary above the port of Looe in 1828. This was connected by a railway with horse traction and granite sleepers to Caradon Moor in 1846. The canal was largely replaced by a railway in 1860 which carried freight – in particular, granite and metallic ores – right down to Looe Quay, thus eliminating transhipment in and out of the canal barges. From 1879 passengers were carried from Moorswater, the station for Liskeard, to Looe. Three intermediate stations in succession were opened, the last being St Keyne, opened in 1902. In the previous year, a connection had been constructed to the GW main line at Liskeard and in 1909 the GW took over the working of both the Liskeard and Caradon and the Liskeard and Looe Railways. The Liskeard and Caradon was closed at the end of 1916. The Liskeard and Looe was closed to freight in 1963 but remains open for passengers.

Stone blocks for securing the rails were commonly used for horse railways, and in the early days of steam railways. (Among others, the Stockton and Darlington, the Liverpool and Manchester and the London and Birmingham made use of stone sleepers.) Their lack of resilience was one of the reasons for their replacement by wooden sleepers, and it is of interest to find granite blocks in use for so long on the Liskeard and Looe. The explanation lies in the availability of granite from the Cheesewring Quarries, on the Caradon Railway. Although from the 1860s steam locomotives were in use, speeds were not of the order at which the unyielding track would be likely to cause cracked rails or broken springs on rolling stock. The photograph shows St Keyne, viewed from the south, before operating was taken over by the GW. The granite blocks are still in use. Although the first locomotive had been introduced in 1860, the erosion of vegetation between the rails would indicate the passage of horses or pedestrians. The bed of the disused canal is on the right and needless to say the bridge, with its arches for railway and canal, is of granite. The station has a granite faced platform, but a corrugated iron shelter with an oil lamp, and a wooden seat and fence posts. However, the special interest lies in the continued use of stone sleepers in the twentieth century.

241 Milepost near Stanhope, (NY 997388), on 5 September 1970

242 Wagon turntables at Exeter, formerly LSWR (SX 917928), on 9 September 1969

Like the turnpike roads and the canals before them, but with rather more consistency, the railways provided mileposts. It was also the practice to place distinctive posts at quarter, half and three-quarter miles, one of their functions being to assist in the identification of particular points on the track. Most of the companies had their own designs, and the example shown is from the North Eastern Railway. The railway reached Stanhope in 1862 and was extended up the Wear Valley to Wearhead in 1895. Closure to passengers occurred in 1953 but the line remains open as far as the cement works at Eastgate, and the series of mileposts is intact to this point.

Some canals and early railways used milestones, but the iron post is almost universal. The NER post, in plan, consisted of a cross, surmounted by a crosspiece to which an appropriate plate could be secured by bolts. In contrast to canals and turnpikes, railways did not usually show where distance was being measured from, because their posts were provided mainly for their own staff, who would be expected to know. However, in some cases the NER did provide this information in abbreviated form, and the plate shown is marked 'W.V.J^c 13', indicating 13 miles from Wear Valley Junction. Different shaped plates were used to distinguish quarter, half and three-quarter mileposts. At present, railway mileposts are well maintained, but metrication may present a threat.

In 1862 the 50 chain connection between the LSW Queen Street Station was opened to the main GW Exeter station at St Davids. It was steeply graded at 1 in 37, as indicated in the photograph by comparing the running lines with the sidings on either side. The bracket signal on the up line is of a conventional design, with metal posts and upper quadrant arms for the platform road and through road in what became Exeter Central Station. However, the signal applying to the siding has a normal lattice post and bracket but a wooden doll with a McKenzie and Holland-type finial and a short, lower quadrant arm. The post bears a cast iron notice as follows: 'Only tank engines of the 044 060 and 062 types may pass over the turntables on No.2 siding. Speed not to exceed 5 m.p.h.'. There were three wagon turntables on No.2 siding, with a fourth on the subsidiary siding which appears in the foreground of the photograph. These were a very common feature of sidings where space was limited. With short, relatively light wagons, manual operation presented no problem and, as most shunting was carried out by horses, the difficulty indicated by the notice on the signal post did not arise. At Exeter a total of 5 stub sidings were constructed; four were reached directly from three turntables on No.2 siding and the fifth from the siding in the right hand bottom corner of the photograph. The latter was aligned at right angles so that it was possible to provide two tracks on the turntable, and wagons could run directly on to it from either direction. The two locking devices are visible on the circumference and stop blocks prevent overrunning. In contrast, the turntable on No.2 siding has only one track, normally aligned with the main siding. This is provided with single stop blocks, sited to catch one side of the wagon, as compared to the double stops for the turntable in the foreground. With the passage of time many wagon turntables stiffened with declining use, and moderate pressure on a wagon standing on them no longer sufficed to move them. Whereas locomotive turntables were useful for turning steam locomotives round, wagon turntables were only used for changing direction. With the advent of longer wagons and the departure of railway horses, they have vanished from the railway scene.

243 LCDR Chair on the Faversham Quay branch, (TR 023616), in April 1955; 244 IWR Chair, not in use, on 24 July 1976; 245 BHR Chair, not in use, on 24 July 1976; 246 LER Chair on the Bowes Railway, (NZ 275574), on 6 August 1978; 247 MetR Chair on the Bowes Railway, (NZ 277576), on 6 August 1978; 248 GWR Chair, not in use, on 24 July 1976

With the adoption of new types of track, chairs are no longer used for fixing rails to sleepers. A group of six are illustrated, indicating the increase in weight corresponding to the increased weight of rails. No.243 shows a two hole chair made for the London Chatham and Dover Railway in 1876. The wooden key, used for securing the rail in the chair is just visible at the top, and appears to be rotting away. Chairs were usually fixed to wooden sleepers by screwing in threaded bolts, and the top of one of these is shown.

The Isle of Wight Railway chair (No.244) is dated 1885 and also carries the makers initials: HW & Co'. The LCD design incorporated four webs to support the sides of the chair, but the IWR design has only two. The two bolt holes are offset from the centre line.

The Bexley Heath Railway chair of 1891 (No.245) is somewhat similar in design to the IWR example, with the maker's initials, WP & Co, adjoining the date. Incidentally, the Bexley Heath Railway was operated by the South Eastern Railway and was not opened until 1895.

The Bowes Railway, despite its situation in County Durham, has examples of chairs from three London undertakings: the London Electric, the Metropolitan and the London Passenger Transport Board. The date on the

London Electric Railway chair (No.246) is not clear but looks like 1931. A batch number appears, probably as an alternative to the initials of the manufacturers. In this design there is a double web on one side, resembling the early LCD style, but a very small central web on the other. Three bolt holes were provided, although in the example in use on the Bowes Railway only two were in use. For many years keys were made of wood, but this one is of metal. The London Electric Railway, which was formed in 1910 to operate a number of underground tube lines in London, was absorbed by the London Passenger Transport Board in 1933. It was not unusual for rails, chairs and sleepers to be re-used after removal from running lines, although the move from a London tube tunnel to a colliery line in County Durham must have been a rare one.

The Metropolitan Railway chair (No.247) is similar in design to the example from the LER, with the date (1931), the batch reference and the railway company's name in similar positions. Two of the three holes are occupied by fixing bolts without screw threads, and the key is missing. A nut and bolt securing a fish plate is visible but this, of course, is unconnected with the chair.

The Great Western chair (No.248), although only provided with two bolt holes, is the heaviest of the six. As each side is reinforced with two webs and the holes are on the centre line, it has more in common with the LCD chair of 1876 than the later designs. It has more information on it than any of the other chairs. This includes the initials of the company – GWR; the date of April 1942 – 4-42; the batch number – 95; and the manufacturer's initials – P & P. After the advent of British Railways, bullhead rail in chairs gave place initially to flat bottomed track, and the manufacture of chairs ceased.

249 Notice boards at Carlisle Citadel Station (NY 403555) on 21 June 1937

Carlisle Citadel Station, one of the principal junctions on the West Coast Main Line, was completed in 1848 and operated by the Citadel Station Committee. The LNWR and the Caledonian were both represented on the Committee, but the station was also used by Midland, North Eastern, North British, Glasgow and South Western, and Mayport and Carlisle companies. Through trains to Scotland were operated by the LNWR and the Caledonian, and by the Midland in association with the NB and the GSWR, but it was usual to change locomotives at Carlisle. The notice boards gave train information under the headings DUE and MINUTES LATE, the three columns under the latter allowing for reports from three points along the line. The joint owners of the station used a pair of boards, with the Caledonian allotting some space to the North Eastern trains from Newcastle. All Caledonian trains approaching Carlisle were up trains and all LNW were down, so that the headings to the boards seem rather unnecessary. This view is confirmed by the omission of this information from the boards of the Midland, GSW and NB companies. It was evidently felt that as the Maryport and Carlisle was operating a local service, information about the running of its trains was not required. The Caledonian and North Eastern boards seem to be up to date, unlike the board for the LNWR.

The photograph also shows the wooden fender protecting the wall from the wheels of trolleys on the slope in front of the board, and the massive blocks, terminated by the finely moulded stone forming one side of the doorway. Through the door part of an ex-LNW coach is visible, and also part of an enamelled advertisement which included the word 'established'. Needless to say train information is now displayed with far more sophisticated equipment than blackboard and chalk. It is a little surprising that the Carlisle boards, with the names of the pre-grouping companies serving Carlisle, should have still been in use 14 years after the grouping.

250, 251 Awning brackets supporting platform canopies at Shanklin (SZ 581819) on 12 May 1965, and at Dymock (SO 699310) on 25 July 1971

The Isle of Wight Railway was opened from Ryde as far as Shanklin in 1864. Shanklin was one of the busiest stations on the line and was later extended, with a generous provision of cover for the wide down platform. Its roof was supported by columns with elaborate brackets incorporating ornamental ironwork. The central feature was a ring encircling a monogram consisting of the letters IWR. The rest of the space was filled with iron foliage and flowers. With the present tendency to simplify stations and remove buildings and platform canopies, ironwork of this kind is at risk, but at the time of writing the Shanklin example still survives.

This is not the case at Dymock. The Newent Railway was opened from Over Junction near Gloucester through Newent to Dymock in 1885. An extension by the Ross and Ledbury company on to Ledbury was opened at the same time and both companies were absorbed by the GWR in 1892. At Dymock the platform canopy was not supported by columns as at Shanklin but heavy wooden beams, strengthened with metal plates, were cantilevered out from the wall of the station building. These were re-inforced with brackets, similar but rather simpler than those at Shanklin.

There was no intricate monogram, but the letters NR appeared on a shield fixed to iron scrollwork. Dymock was closed to passengers in 1959 and has now been demolished.

252, 253 Platform seats at Lewisham (TQ 381759) in January 1955, and at Canning Town (TQ 393816) on 2 May 1964

Lewisham, on the North Kent line of the South Eastern Railway, was opened in 1849 and continues to handle a considerable passenger traffic. The practice of providing shelter and seats for waiting passengers on platforms, to supplement waiting rooms, was certainly well established by the late-Victorian period. The seats had to withstand weather and heavy use and were usually wooden with iron legs. The SE example from Lewisham has ends of strap iron fixed to a seat made up of wooden cross-pieces. The initial letters SER were made of cast iron and fixed to the strap iron. They had no structural function but combined the roles of a property marker and a discrete advertisement. It will be seen that to prevent damage to the platform, the legs were fixed to wooden battens.

Canning Town was on the Eastern Counties and Thames Junction Railway, which was opened in 1846 and extended to North Woolwich in 1847. Its importance increased rapidly with the construction of the Royal Docks system, and it was quadrupled between Stratford South Junction and Tidal Basin. Photograph No.253 shows the separate freight lines at the back of the platform. The development of road traffic and the decline of the docks have combined to reduce rail traffic, but Canning Town is still open. The GER platform seat may be compared with the SER example. The legs are of heavier, cast iron, and there are no arms. A single plank provides the seat, and two more make a back. A monogram is incorporated in the end. The names of stations were given on nameboards, on lamp cases and, on some lines – as shown at Canning Town – on the backs of seats. Plates were removed during the invasion scare of 1940 and not many were replaced. (Other companies painted over the name, and in the same way, these were not all repainted after the war.) The photograph also shows the railings at the back of the platform, and a heavy porter's trolley propped against a post. Although taken in 1964, it could equally well have been taken in 1922.

254, 255, 256 Warning notices at Durley (SU 526151) on 13 April 1964, Pontyates (SN 470082) on 25 September 1965 and at Ulverston (SD 285779) on 13 April 1966

The branch line from Botley to Bishops Waltham in Hampshire was opened in 1863, closed to passengers at the end of 1932 and to all traffic in 1962. The level crossing at Durley was unmanned but was well-provided with warning notices. There were three on the west side of the line. An 'L & SWR Beware of Trains' warning is visible in the background of the first view, but the notice in the foreground is more unusual. Headed 'London & South Western Railway', it read as follows: 'In order to ensure as far as possible the safety not only of trains running on the railway but also of the persons and traffic entitled to use this occupation crossing notice of the intention to pass traction and other road engines through this gate and over the railway must be previously given to the company's servants at the nearest station. Godfrey Knight, Secretary'. There remains some doubt as to whether road engine drivers always did walk about $1\frac{1}{2}$ miles to Botley Station before crossing the single line.

The iron notice of the BP & GV Railway is more conventional. Painting over with black paint rather obscures the wording which is as follows: 'Burry Port and Gwendreath Valley Railway. Notice. Under the provision of the Tenth Section of the Burry Port and Gwendreath Valley Railway Light Railway Extension Order 1911 any person who shall trespass upon any of the railways of the company referred to in such order shall on conviction be liable to a penalty not exceeding forty shillings and in accordance with the provisions of the said Order public warning is hereby given to all persons not to trespass upon the said railways. By Order'. Although of conventional design and dimensions the BP&GV notice lacks the name of a senior official and a date. The line was opened in 1869 but the notice was erected after 1911, by which time iron castings were giving place to enamel.

An unusual feature of the Furness Railway notice is the way it has been painted with black letters on a white background, in contrast to the normal white letters on a black background. The text is conventional: 'Persons trespassing upon the railways belonging to the Furness Railway company are liable to a penalty of Forty Shillings under the Furness Railway Act 1894, and, in accordance with the provisions of the said Act, public warning is hereby given, to all persons, not to trespass upon the said railways. May 1904. By Order'. Although notices were usually fixed to a post at points where trespass was likely to occur, the Furness notice was secured to a wall. Examples of notices already illustrated include the GW bilingual notice (photograph No.210), the elaborate I&AJ Railway pronouncement of 1858 (Nos.232 and 233) and the GNSR enamelled notice of 1909 (No.237).

257, 258, 259, 260, 261, 262 Property marks at Stratford (TQ 387848) on 21 May 1964, at Swansea (SS 676929) on 7 August 1974, at Gravesend (TQ 646744) on 1 May 1971, at Cheltenham (SO 938224) on 6 June 1968, at Purfleet (TQ 554783) on 29 March 1959, and at Whitstable (TR 110671) on 24 August 1973

In some cases, property marks did no more than mark boundaries but occasionally, like the initials on platform seats or roof brackets, there was an informatory aspect which bordered on advertisement. The Great Eastern example from Stratford (No.257), fixed to a wall of the railway works, had a legal and an informatory function.

The Great Western used a disc to mark property boundaries (No.258), usually mounted horizontally on a length of bridge rail. The words 'Great Western Railway Co' appeared on the circumference, and in the centre 'Boundary' and the date; in the example shown this was 1908. This particular mark indicated the boundary between land owned by the GW and that of the Swansea Harbour Trustees. After 1923, when the GW acquired the docks, it became of historic interest only.

The LTSR marked the limit of their property at Gravesend with stone rather than metal, with a design which would appear to owe something to a parish boundary stone (No.259). Although the lines of the LTSR were confined to the Essex side, they always regarded Gravesend, on the Kent side of the Thames, as part of their territory. They served the town with ferry steamers and for many years passenger boats used the Town Pier, which was owned by Gravesend Corporation, while cattle and, later, motor carrying boats used West Street Pier which was owned by the LTS. At the present time, only passenger boats are operating, and only West Street is in use for ferry services.

The elaborate GWR monogram appeared on an iron gate at Malvern Road Station in Cheltenham (No.260). This was a comparatively late station, opened in 1906 and closed in 1966. It belonged to a period when economy was already to be observed in establishments such as halts, but at Malvern Road the expense of adding the company's initials to gates was considered appropriate.

However, even in the palmiest days it was unusual to mark fences, and the plate at Purfleet (No.261), on the LTSR, is a rare example.

Gate plates are no longer produced but the example from Whitstable Harbour (No.262) is at least as recent as the SE&C Joint Committee of 1899. Now of little direct use, it continues to provide information for the railway historian.

263, 264 Knockholt, formerly SECR (TQ 485629), in 1922, and an SECR signal finial, not in use

The view at Knockholt shows how characteristic of particular companies signalling equipment could be. The signal cabin, with its hipped roof and sash windows, bears the unmistakable stamp of the South Eastern Railway. The weather-boarded construction and the platform, used for both window cleaning and for the signalman to exhibit flags when necessary, are also characteristic. The name-plate lettered 'Knockholt Station Signals' was another distinctive feature. The up starter, on the left, is typical of the SECR but incorporates SE features, such as the white circle instead of the usual band on the arm of the stop signal. In order to improve sighting the arm was placed on a doll supported on a bracket, but the reason for a bracket on the left as well as the right is less obvious. It may form a counterbalance in a location in which it was difficult to place a wire to secure the post in position. Other signalling features include the rodding for the points, the wires for the signals and, in the background, a tall home signal post. The train is a down continental boat express consisting mainly of Pullman cars. The train locomotive appears to belong to the SEC D1 class and the pilot is D class No.748. This was built by the Vulcan Foundry in 1903 and withdrawn in 1951. Both locomotives are in the post war livery of the SECR with their numbers in large numerals on the tenders.

The size of railway equipment is not always appreciated, and so photograph No.263 shows a finial of the type on the signal in No.262, related to a foot rule. The initials SECR are just visible. Needless to say, modern colour light signals are less varied than their semaphore predecessors.

162

265 Automatic machine at Shanklin (SZ 581819) on 12 May 1968

Automatic machines began to appear on station platforms around the turn of the century. These were not owned by the railway companies but in nearly all cases were the property of the British Automatic Company, who paid a rental for the sites. Vending and weighing machines were to be found on all well-frequented stations, but a less obvious facility was the machine which printed your name – or anything else – on a metal strip. An example from Shanklin is shown in original condition. The initials of the BAC appear, with a list of their main offices in London, Manchester, Bristol, Glasgow, Dublin and Brussels. One of the operating levers released the pointer and the other stamped the metal plate, which was delivered through the hole in the front of the machine. The Out of Order notice is suspended from the slot for the insertion of pennies. Weighing and printing machines have almost disappeared from the railway scene, although vending machines of modern design are still in evidence on the busier stations.

266, 267 Gas pipe cover at Oxford (SP 504063) on 30 April 1966; **water pipe cover** at Buckfastleigh (SX 746663) on 14 April 1973

Many railway companies had their own works, producing gas from oil. This was used mainly for the lighting of coaches and for cooking in restaurant cars. Provision was made for the 'gassing' of coaches in sidings, but also in some stations. Oxford had this facility, with a series of gassing points which could be connected by flexible hose to stationary coaches. The covers were marked GWR OIL GAS and remained in use until gas cooking ended in restaurant cars.

The requirement for water was considerably greater. Water cranes for the replenishment of locomotives have already been mentioned, but there was a more modest requirement for the lavatories of coaches. At present this is usually met at stations by small, wheeled tankers, but examples remain of water points, analogous to gassing points. The cover of one is shown, marked GWR WATER.

268 Table setting in GNR Dining Car on 17 October 1952

The cutlery and crockery of the pre-grouping companies was invariably marked, the need being more obvious than for instance in the case of awning brackets. Initials were always given, but sometimes a coat of arms as well. The table setting illustrated was prepared in a GNR Dining Car for the exhibition to celebrate the centenary of King's Cross Station. The plate in the background came from one of the sets specially produced for sale on the Silver Jubilee express in 1935. Needless to say, silver is now a rarity in dining cars.

269, 270 Wagon and axle box cover at Newport (SZ 499896) on 9 May 1964

This view shows a 4-wheel bolster wagon with a hand-operated brake. Although not in use for normal traffic when the photograph was taken, there have been few changes, and the clip for securing the destination details is still in position. Buffing gear and springs remain unchanged, but passenger-type screw couplings have replaced the normal chain links. Of particular interest are the axle box covers, still lettered LB & SCRy.

271, 272 Horses at Whitstable Harbour (TR 110672) on 20 April 1939, and at Ashtead (TQ 181590) in about 1905 (see p. 166)

The railways used thousands of horses, both for shunting and for road deliveries. Their use continued after the Second World War, the last shunting horses being retired from Newmarket in 1967. They wore a fairly conventional harness and were hitched to the chain-link couplings on wagons. As they usually walked between the rails, when two were required they double-headed in the same way as locomotives. Braking was the responsibility of the shunter, using the wagon brakes. The first photograph shows a pair of horses moving an 8-plank coal wagon at Whitstable Harbour. (Also visible is a weighted point lever.)

The railways made considerable use of agents for their cartage services, and although it is marked 'LSWR Ashtead', the horse and cart in the second photograph was the property of an agent. In this carefully posed photograph the station master is checking the load. Both horse and cart are lighter than those operated by the companies. The passenger station is in the background. Horses have now completely disappeared from the British railways, not only as sources of traction but, since the withdrawal of horse boxes, as sources of revenue as well.

Index